David duChemin

A Beautiful Anarchy

When the Life Creative
Becomes the Life Created

rockynook

A Beautiful Anarchy:
When the Life Creative Becomes the Life Created
David duChemin
www.davidduchemin.com

Project editor: Ted Waitt
Project manager: Lisa Brazieal
Marketing manager: Jessica Tiernan
Layout and type: Kim Scott, Bumpy Design
Cover design: Kim Scott, Bumpy Design and David duChemin
Cover title illustration: James Victore
Cover image © Manoch Sridakest / Shutterstock
Back cover author photo: Adam Blasberg

ISBN: 978-1-68198-234-2
1st Rocky Nook Edition (2nd printing, June 2020)
© 2017 David duChemin

Rocky Nook Inc.
1010 B Street, Suite 350
San Rafael, CA 94901
USA

www.rockynook.com

Distributed in the UK and Europe by Publishers Group UK
Distributed in the U.S. and all other territories by Ingram Publisher Services

Library of Congress Control Number: 2016957327

Printed in the USA

"Life isn't about finding yourself.
Life is about creating yourself."
~ George Bernard Shaw

For Cynthia,
My Beautiful Anarchist

CONTENTS

FOREWORD

"When was the last time you failed?" This is a frequent question asked of me. I don't know if my answer is jacked up on hubris…but I do know it's honest—"Every day."

As an artist and designer, it's my job to tempt failure every day. It's not that I'm looking to stumble or am seeking financial ruination, but not tempting failure would lead to me finding a gimmick, a trick that people like—then rolling that trick out again and again and again. Society tells us this is good—the *goal* even. But "people pleasing" leads to losing your own way and, ultimately, boredom. It's my job to make myself happy, to make work I love and, if I do a good job, others will love it as well. Or they won't—hence, tempting failure every day, but I'd rather risk it all on love every day because love always pays off.

With love,
James Victore

A BEAUTIFUL ANARCHY

The word "anarchy" literally means "without a ruler." In popular use, it's a political word with heavy baggage, a bloody history, and occasional car bombs. This book is not about that: it's about freedom.

This is a book about the freedom to create—to live a life of unapologetic, passionate, daring creation—in whatever arena resonates best for you. Parents create when they raise a child, entrepreneurs create when they begin a business, and teachers create when they design a lesson plan. Some people identify with the urge to create more than others, and it's to them I speak in this book, not because others can't benefit, but because anyone who persists in the idea that "I'm just not really creative" is unlikely to read this book, believing instead that the die has been cast and they've been excluded. They, of all people, need most to read it, and I hope they do.

This book is for people who have a sense of their own urge to create, or those who don't but long to look under the hood and find it waiting there. But to its bones, this is a book about art and the process of making it, because what is our life but a chance to make the greatest art of all? Whether you ever set your paintbrush on actual canvas isn't remotely the point, though I hope you will. What is very much the point is that each of us is given a canvas—from one edge to the other the span of our life—and each of us has a chance to do something brilliant with it. Each of us has the chance to fill that canvas with wild, achingly beautiful swirls of colour, and if you're reading this there's a chance that you feel right now that your canvas is empty, or dotted here and there with hesitant, half-hearted stops and starts, the brush pulled up before you could even gain momentum, for fear of doing it wrong.

As I write this introduction to a now half-written book, the sun is rising in Bali. It's August 2013 and a trailer's just come out for a movie version of one of my favourite short stories, *The Secret Life of Walter Mitty*. Mitty's a dreamer, working as a photo editor at *LIFE* magazine, allowing daydreams to be a substitute for actually doing what he longs to do. Working at *LIFE*, but never having one. And then he looks at a photograph of a photojournalist in a refugee camp (played by Sean Penn), and the photograph comes to life long enough for Penn's character to gesture an invitation to Mitty. Come. Stop observing. Stop abdicating your life. Live a great story instead of just watching, telling, or dreaming them.

I'm self-conscious about saying it, but I want to be that man; I want to be someone, among many, I hope, who calls to the dreamer and says, "Wake up." I want to invite others to begin living now, not later, and to ask them with a straight face to step out of their comfort zones and face the fear. I want to see every person in my life doing what they long to do, free from the things that hold them back. Life is not in the dreaming, but in the doing. Don't you dare get to the end of your life, your canvas clean and unmarked. There is no prize for the one who leaves his canvas clean, his scribbled signature in the corner the only thing to differentiate his own off-white rectangle of a life from all the million others who—too paralyzed by fear—have done the same.

My massage therapist once told me the stars were aligning auspiciously. She told me it was a good time to dream big dreams. Not one with a particular reverence for the opinions of the stars, I told her I dream big dreams every day; it's up to the universe to keep up. I wasn't being sarcastic, and she knew it. I also wasn't being cocky. I was just being honest. I do believe in dreams; the bigger the better. But I also believe in action. I believe in great ideas, too, but I don't believe coming up with great ideas is the same as being creative. Being creative is about creating. It's about doing. And so too is living, because life is an act of creation. Day by day, whatever else we make, our first act of creation is our own lives. We must first make the artist before we make the art. Out of nothing, nothing comes.

This book is a call to colour outside the lines, in both art and life. It is a book about living free from the rule of everything that holds us back from being the humans we were created to become. It is about living free of the rule, or tyranny, of fear and shame, of debt and obligation, and every "should" or "should not" that we have not willingly signed off on. Your art, the thing that stirs from your heart, mind, and soul, the thing that moves you (and hopefully, others), is a free agent, and the moment you begin to ask, "What *should* I do?" or, "How *should* I do this?" you allow your art to teeter, to lean towards conformity and away from authentic expression.

To do what we *should* in art is bondage. To tell others, with our art, what they *should* think or feel or do is propaganda. And to tell other artists how they *should* do their art, whether that's visual art, the written word, or creating a business, is presumptuous, and unkind, and tells the muse we've learned nothing at all under her influence.

All very well for the artist, but what of the rest of the world, those working a regular job, whatever that means? I think it all applies equally, if not differently, and that there is room (there *must* be room) to live our lives increasingly on our terms, as engaged and intentional as possible, as creatively as possible, with the freedom to follow the muse, or our own curiosity, down the road that's unique to us. I think almost any endeavour undertaken on those terms can be art.

I'm a photographer and author, a publisher, and former comedian. I've made a living from my own creativity since I worked my way through college as a comedian, and while making a living in the arts in no way means my art is *good*, per se, it does mean I've relied on it a little more than I might have otherwise, and I think that dependence on my muse has made us more familiar with each other than I might have been otherwise. To write that my muse and I are familiar, however, is to understate what's happened between us. My muse and I have worked closely together over the last twenty years, and the uneasy relationship has become less turbulent over time. And while I'm never quite sure how she feels about me, I think it's fair—if not overly anthropomorphic and unnecessarily romantic—to say I've fallen in love with her, and the life my creativity has made possible.

There is nothing I would rather do than work creatively and, in so doing, to make a living. Whether making a business, making a photograph, or writing a book, the urge to create has always been central to who I am. I believe it is central to who we all are, which is one of the reasons I get twitchy when I hear someone tell me they "aren't really creative." We're *all* creative, but we've allowed the arts to co-opt that word while making every other area of human creativity feel a little too self-conscious about using it. And I think we've misunderstood the creative process, which if it's anything at all is messy, each successful endeavour hardwon, each masterpiece the result of a hundred failed sketches and many tears.

It's the fundamental creative urge within us that makes otherwise rational people take complete leave of our senses and have children. It's that same urge that compels people to build houses, find cures for diseases, build companies and products, solve complicated mathematical problems, or write music. The same creative urge that compelled the first cave man to draw animals on cave walls is the same urge that compelled him to carve obsidian into arrowheads and hunt those same animals for food and clothing. It is that impulse within us to follow the whispers of our curiosity, or the urgency of our needs, around dark corners and into the unknown, that is responsible for every astonishing advancement in our history—the discovery of fire, the law of gravity, the revolution of the earth around the sun, the evolution of the species, and the creation of Michelangelo's *David*, Picasso's *Guernica*, and Handel's *Messiah*.

For every advancement that has taken place, every creation of some new beauty in some new field, that advancement has taken place as a movement from the known and accepted into the unknown and, at times, unaccepted— to the point of outright rejection. Galileo was declared a heretic for his idea that the earth revolved around the sun and not the other way around. Darwin's never been popular with the same crowd, either. Picasso's cubism was revolutionary and took several years to overcome initial negative reception, even from fellow artists, people who should know better than to hang on so tightly to convention.

Of course, public reaction, either negative or positive, is not the point. The point is that the long history of creativity—in every imaginable field—takes us inevitably into places where we have to pour new wine into old wineskins, and that invites criticism, which in turn invites fear, and soon we're back to hiding in the shadows, letting others take the risk while we abdicate the responsibility to do the one great thing we can do with our lives—be fully ourselves and make art of our lives.

This book is an invitation to celebrate the life creative, and in so doing to embrace its essential and beautiful anarchy. I use the word "anarchy" metaphorically rather than politically, as a call to live our lives on our own terms, which is the only way we can fully be ourselves. It's a call to live our lives free from the bondage of *should* and *ought to*: the only way to be truly alive. We need more of these kinds of anarchists, more people who understand the extraordinary beauty and brevity of life, and who daily find the courage to follow that voice that calls them to something more, even when they don't know what that *something more* is. Even when that voice calls them to places beyond the points that other voices say they should turn back.

What we do not need is anarchy for anarchy's sake. I value this thin metaphor of anarchy because I think, as a metaphor, it represents a beautiful way of life, and of thinking about the creative process and our lives-as-art. When I chose to use this metaphor I did so because it works for me. This beautiful anarchy is not about freedom from law, nor my own desire to live with, or without, certain rules. But where I do embrace rules, they are rules I have myself signed off on because they resonate with me, they make the world a better place and are, I hope, descriptive of my life, not prescriptive. I've chosen to live by the rule of love, kindness, and respect—toward others and myself. I believe in forgiveness and grace and, so far as it aligns with my conscience, the law of the land. I pay my taxes. I believe in being a responsible citizen. In fact, I believe the life this metaphor describes makes me a better global citizen, and a better human being. If the metaphor fails for you, then find one that works, so long as it leads you to the freedom and joy of creation, and of doing so in the most authentic way possible.

Whatever metaphor you choose, I hope this book gives you the courage to begin filling your canvas again, and if you reach down for the brush only to find it hardened from lack of use, then throw it away and plunge your hands into the paint. However you have to do it, don't leave your canvas blank. Don't deprive your soul, and the people around you, of the chance to see you fill every inch of that canvas—messy and wildly human as it might be—with every flaming colour.

LIFE IS SHORT

That life is short is so blindingly obvious to most of us that it's become a cliché. I'm not sure where the line between truth and cliché is, but it's thin. And I'm not sure that we can be free of the truth of things, or free from the chance to act on them, merely by calling them cliché. Sometimes I wonder if we call things cliché in order to excuse ourselves from thinking about them.

Our days are numbered, folks. Not only are they limited, we have no idea exactly how many days remain in the storehouse. Our time here is not merely a resource to be managed. It is *all* we have, and it's insanely beautiful at times, but it's *short.*

One of the gifts of photography is the way it makes us conscious of time. Time is one of our raw materials. Our exposures are measured, in part, in fractions of a second. Sometimes so fast the shutter is closed before you know it's open. The best photographs also rely on the strength, beauty, and universality of a particular *moment*. Blink and it's gone, but when photographed it remains, frozen in space and time, to consider for as long as the print remains. Photography helps those who are willing to see the moments we'd otherwise miss. And moments are important because the way we live our moments is the way we live our days, our lives. Photographs—the best of them, at any rate—honour the moments, and they speak to us because we know how limited these moments are. Time is limited and we've no idea how much of it we have, so the sooner we cherish and redeem it, the better.

Time is not money. If time were money we could borrow it. We could steal it. We could bank it and see our days compounded. We can't. We can live it. We can use it to do the thing we are here for, or we can waste it. But we can do little else with it because it's not ours to control. It's given to us in unspecified measure to wring from it what we can.

I am strongly motivated by the brevity of life, not because I fear its end (though like Woody Allen, I'd rather achieve immortality by not dying than through my work), but because, simply, it will end. What I control is how deeply I live my days, not how long. But I think somewhere along the way the urge to live deeply gets subverted.

We settle. We find a path of lesser resistance and we take the deal, because it's easier to be safe. It's easier to fit in. We'd rather tiptoe through life and make it safely through, because we seem to have willingly forgotten that there's no reward in making it unscathed to our funeral.

Why we take the deal in the first place is another discussion to be had later, because it's got a lot to do with fear and the voices we listen to, but it's important to realize we've settled. There's not a week goes by that someone doesn't tell me they envy my life (and by that they usually mean the good bits, the public bits of my story; few have told me they desperately want to take the path I've taken to get here) and that they wish they could do what I do. And I get it. I really do. But what they seem to mean is that they want what I have without paying the price I've paid to get here. I know people want to change the world and create great art and live the dream and so on. So do I. But some want to do so without giving up what is demanded, by life, in exchange. Were life longer I might have time to do it all, but I don't, and so I make choices: do I do this, or do I do that? Seldom am I given a choice to do both. I don't own a home. My freedom from mortgage payments and maintenance issues frees me to travel. Some can do both. I can't. I've made a choice. I'd rather have a plane ticket to Bali than a big screen television.

But to the one who sees no choice but to keep up with their neighbors, the television comes first and the plane ticket remains a dream. For me, if owning the latest car or appliance means I give up the experience of travel, and the freedom to do my work, it comes at too high a cost. Most of us love the idea of having a choice until we're told that choice means giving up one to have another. Some don't realize it is a choice.

Life will go by so fast it'll make our aged heads spin when we get to the end. But it's not only short, it's uncertain. When I graduated from high school we were already talking about careers and what we'd do when we retired. Not once did we say, "*If* we retire"—we treated it as a given. We would retire and in health enough to enjoy the dreams we'd set aside for that retirement. But life has this way of getting in the way of deferred dreams. Leukemia arrives uninvited. A headache becomes a brain tumour that becomes a fight against a possibility we never imagined until it's clear the dreams we saved for later will never happen. I don't mean to be morbid but we live, many of us, in a culture that lives in perpetual denial of the inevitable, and it's costing us our dreams. You can't bank your time. The time, as it has always been, is only now.

That my days are numbered forces me to choose carefully how I spend them. And because my life—even if I live to 120—will seem so heartbreakingly short, I will choose not only *what* I do with my life, but *how* I do it.

I know. It sounds so selfish. We've been taught to keep our heads down. We've been taught not to be selfish. Many of us are also taught to respect the choices of others, and to give them the dignity of living their lives on their own terms. We're taught to extend forgiveness, to be kind. We're taught to love others as we love ourselves. But the moment we try to love ourselves the way we're taught to love others we're chastised: "Don't be so selfish."

And yes, sometimes they're right. But often they aren't, and the admonition against selfishness has become a perverse reversal of things. The most loving people I know find that love *first* within themselves. It is the self-loathing who abhor others. It's the ones who won't respect themselves that don't respect others. It is the ones who don't allow themselves to risk and dream and live extraordinary, unconventional lives who discourage others from the same.

At the risk of being misunderstood, I think it's time we took back a healthy regard for selfishness. In fact, I'll go one better (in for a penny, in for a pound, right?): I think it's time we made ourselves a priority. To do otherwise is to expect a bountiful yield from a garden we've neither planted nor tended. I'm not suggesting we allow ourselves to become egomaniacs, just that we extend the same love and grace to ourselves that we do to others, and to do so *first* so we have a place from which to love and respect others. That we respect ourselves and allow ourselves the same chance to live our dreams as we allow others. Only when we take back the responsibility to make our own choices—to live on our terms—do we have a place for extraordinary generosity, profound kindness, and the acts of heroism of which we're capable, and of which others will one day call *selfless*.

I'm not looking to justify a life of what I would have once called selfishness; I'm looking for a healthy place to put myself in this world. A place to stand. A place from which to love and do what I have been called, by Life, to do. A place to do good, to love boldly and without fear. A place to be generous and hospitable, and to create my art without shame in the days I have allotted to me. A place to become everything I can be, without settling for anything less. A place from which I can find the leverage to make the same things happen in the lives of those I love. Life is too short to do anything else, and too beautiful not to fight hard to be a part of it.

EX NIHILO

There is an old Latin saying that gets thrown around in the theological circles from which I emerged as a young man when I left college: *ex nihilo nihil fit.* "Out of nothing, nothing comes." Its use, as far as doctrine goes, is to enforce the idea of a Prime Mover. Nothing comes from nothing, so before there was something, there must have been Something Else to create the something. Or something like that. The years have taken most of the details from the dogma of which I was once fond, and smoothed my edges a little. But the idea remains sound, at least as a metaphor.

I'm listening to Miles Davis's *Kind of Blue* album right now, the cover of which was shot by photographer Jay Maisel. That's neither here nor there, but the following story is. As the story goes, a student approached Jay and asked him, "How do I make more interesting photographs?" Without pausing, Jay replied, "Become a more interesting person." Indeed.

We are the source of our own creations, whether that's a story, a child, a photograph, or a business. That work of art, if it's to be art at all (and I think all of those can be), will reflect the artist in some fashion. So then the act of creation that is our first concern is ourselves. Before we create art, we must create the artist. I think it's fair to talk in these terms, forgetting for a moment that on the surface it sounds profoundly narcissistic, because I don't believe we're just passive victims of fate. Yes, life happens to us in ways we never expected, and luck, or serendipity, has a way about it that's hard not to see as wondrous and mysterious (as well as cruel and malign) much of the time. But we live and create in reaction to these events, and it is those reactions over which we have control.

When the potter is given a lump of clay, he creates something of it—either passively, by doing nothing and letting it harden into a useless block, or actively, by putting it on the wheel and shaping it to his desire. We are what we are, flaws and all—and I'll talk about the power of constraints later—but what we are *not* is powerless. As our history on this planet too well illustrates, the human will is powerful, and the decision to react to what life brings us is either a creative force or a destructive one in our all-too-short lives. It's by virtue of the will to react and make choices—even in the light of some very dark, or paralyzing, circumstances—that we create our own lives.

As a photographer, I am a vocal advocate of a very intentional approach to making photographs. There are a lot of decisions that affect the final outcome of the image, and I think abdicating those decisions is a lost opportunity to create something that more clearly expresses ourselves. I believe the same about life.

In fact, I believe this so strongly that I would like to try one more metaphor. As a race we've found meaning in stories for millennia. We consume stories at an astonishing rate. What stories we choose to read, watch, or listen to become a part of us. Sadly, because they do give meaning, I suspect many of these stories have become a substitute for living an interesting life. Stripped of all risk, it's easier to *watch* great stories than to *live* them. But choose to live a great story, and we open ourselves to all the possibilities the human drama has always drawn on. Exciting, heady stuff to find the love of your life, but it comes with the risk of heartache and loss. Easier, perhaps, to curl up with whatever movie in which Tom Hanks and Meg Ryan's characters are falling in love than to do so ourselves. Amazing to jump on a plane to Africa or Southeast Asia for an adventure, but you risk all the uncertainties that have kept thousands from doing the same thing, safe at home on the couch instead with their Lonely Planet book and BBC travel documentaries.

We have the choice to actively write a more interesting story or passively accept the one that comes our way. I'd be contradicting myself to say we *ought* to choose one over the other. Part of being human is having the dignity to choose. But if our lives are stories then it's the more interesting one that I'd rather both read and write. And it's the person living that more interesting story that is going to create the most interesting, meaningful art with their life. That kind of life happens intentionally. We may not choose the things that happen to us—few of us do—but we control our own reactions and, in that way, shape the clay we've been given.

So much of our raw material lies outside our grasp. None of us controls what is behind us in our past. We don't control the parents to whom we were born, or the place or income bracket in which we grew up. We went to this or that school, and by the time we turn 18 we've had a childhood of victories and defeats, joys and sorrows, and enough traumas, either real or imagined, to fuel a life-time of angst-ridden dreams or novels, should we decide to pay it forward and inflict those on future generations. We will, because this is life, continue to collect these experiences. But they are raw materials only, and what we do with them is a part of the choices we make in the creation of ourselves. It's a collaborative effort with Life, an unpredictable partner to be sure, but it's our *reactions* that form the people we become.

To those reactions we add our choices about the stories we listen to, the books we read, the people with whom we surround ourselves, and the jobs in which we choose to remain too long. We choose the ones to whom we give our hearts, our time, our money. We choose to continue learning or not. We choose to buy that new stereo instead of the ticket to Australia for the year in the outback we always wanted. And in so doing, we create the person we become, piece by piece. It's a good argument for making those decisions with greater care and intention.

If I've got a tendency to oversimplify, forgive me; I know life is profoundly complicated at times. But I also know that "it's complicated" is a poor excuse for resigning ourselves to our fate, as though it's our lot in life. It would be easy to allow overwhelming debt, bankruptcy, divorce, a diabetes diagnosis, or a near-fatal fall that shatters both your feet, to sideline you. Or me. I've lived through all of those, and there have been times I'd have thrown all this right back in the face of anyone who told me excitedly that I was "living a really great story." But they'd be right all the same, and at the end of it, what have we got but to make the best of it, and write the best damn story we can? Self-pity makes an interesting scene in the movie, especially when it leads to broken furniture, a bar fight, or preferably both—but it gets old fast, and after a few minutes it's neither a story we want to keep watching, nor one we want to be a part of. The best stories are never the easy ones.

I keep using the word *react* but it's only half the story; living in reaction, even mindful reaction, is not living intentionally. Take your favourite story: the hero usually resists the initial call to adventure, or love. Then something comes along to force him into the fray—he reacts and embarks. But at a certain point the story becomes his own, and it is his desire that drives him forward, not just circumstances. He eventually risks it all because the calling now comes not from outside voices or forces, but from deep inside. Now might be a good time to start unabashedly asking yourself, "*What do I want?*"

Some of the best stories don't really begin until the hero grapples with that question. And for some of us the grappling will come hard because we've been taught not to ask the question. It seems selfish. But I think the things we do in life that are motivated by desire and love are the most powerful, and I don't believe that our happiness has to come at the expense of others. I believe we're connected and my happiness has to include that of others. I'll talk more about this, but I want to plant the question. The first question is not, "What should I be doing with my life?" It's, "What do I want to do with my life?" And if that sounds selfish to some, I can only say that it's in identifying the deepest desires of my heart or mind that I find my calling. It's my hardwiring, and I believe it was put there by Something or Someone good.

Knowing, deep down, what you want to do with your life leads to a ruthless prioritization of resources. Knowing your time, among other resources, is limited, and knowing what you want to do with that time, allows you a profound freedom, even if that freedom is not always easy.

If you want to create more interesting, meaningful, beautiful songs, paintings, businesses, or meals, become a more interesting, meaningful, and beautiful person. Gather the best raw materials you can (or the only ones you've got), work within the constraints you're handed, and make something new. The art comes from the will of the artist, but first there has to be an artist, and—out of nothing, nothing comes. Reaction only takes us so far: it's more a posture of daily life, one we assume while we go about intentionally pursuing, or creating, the things we most long for.

What do you want to do with your life? I don't mean this abstractly or obliquely. Find some silence and sit down with a cup of coffee. Mindfully consider your life now, the things you've done with your life that have made you the most content or fulfilled. What do you want to be remembered for, one day long in the future when your moments run out? Write it down. What does your heart long for? What dreams can you not let go of? What obstacles stand in the way now? What steps could you take to clear them? If those desires are worth pursuing, they're worth recognizing and clearing a path for.

THE ARTIST'S JOURNEY

One of the great revelations of my life came when I discovered Joseph Campbell and his book *The Hero with a Thousand Faces*. I read it while studying films and screenplays and trying to understand what makes a great story. And I read it while in the middle of a divorce and unsure I would survive the trauma of that.

While challenging to read, I found one idea that stuck with me and resonated so completely that it's still a rare month that I haven't gone back to it, to sift through the paradigm and find meaning. That idea is the Hero's Journey—the idea that in the mythology of every culture through time there are common elements in the stories that give our lives meaning. Books like *The Writer's Journey* by Christopher Vogler and *Story* by Robert McKee explore this idea in order to help writers create stories that are more powerfully resonant. I think we can use the idea to see the creative process from a new perspective, and to write our own story in more intentional ways, and with greater understanding.

The Hero's Journey is not a formula, and it's not prescriptive. It's descriptive. It looks into the stories we've told each other since the dawn of time and asks why they have such a ring of truth, and what elements they have in common. The hero takes many forms, and is not gender specific. She can be a warrior, to be sure, but as often can be an explorer, an inventor, a mother, a tradesman, or an artist. What he or she is is not important; the Hero's Journey is more concerned about the path the hero takes.

Borrowing from the language of Vogler's *The Writer's Journey* (because he makes the often difficult language of Campbell much more accessible), the Hero's Journey begins in the Ordinary World. It is the place in which we live our ordinary lives, waking daily to our ordinary tasks, and from which the hero is about to be shaken by the Call to Adventure (which I'm capitalizing to make it a little easier to see the structure). That call comes in a million ways, but is almost always an awakening, a desire, a longing, or a crazy idea. For me it's often expressed as a "What if...?" However it comes, it's a call away from the mundane: a call to rock a boat, to change a status that's been quo for too long, a call to make—to create—a change.

If you're like me or like most others (including the protagonists in millennia of stories), you're likely to refuse the call at first. The Refusal of the Call is common, and though there are times it's taken up quickly and without thought, it's the human tendency to prefer the familiar and the safe over the unknown. And so we turn our attention elsewhere; we make excuses; we procrastinate. Even when the call itself seems so right and fills a longing, it's our nature to count to three a few times to build the bravado needed to jump into water we know will be cold and dark. Once we own that call, once we accept and dive in, pack our bags, sit down at the typewriter, or get out a new canvas, the journey truly begins. Acceptance of the call is, in most movies, where the action begins and the protagonist crosses the First Threshold into the special world of the adventure, the new world in which the story unfolds and after which nothing will be the same. Dorothy steps onto the Yellow Brick Road, Luke joins the Rebel forces, and Peter Parker puts on the Spider-Man costume for the first time. Here the hero meets allies and enemies, encounters tests and trials, and begins his approach to the Inmost Cave.

The Inmost Cave is where the hero endures the ordeal that is central to the story, the conflict around which the story revolves. Without conflict there is no story. There is no catalyst to change, and no reason for us to keep reading. Who wants to read a story in which there is no conflict? No one. Because life is not like that. We seldom get what we want without struggle and loss. We do not become who we want to become—the best versions of ourselves—without passing through the fire. We do not write the book without tearing up a few pages, nor paint the masterpiece without ruining a few canvases. We know that. It's why the truly epic stories have so endured; we know the best stories, the ones that most resonate with our humanity and fuel our hopes, are the ones that remind us that the harder the struggle, the greater the reward. And it's no token struggle, either. The losses we accumulate on the way can be almost catastrophic, and there are times we're not sure the hero will make it. We don't know the book will get finished, let alone feel right when it does. We don't know our marriage will make it, our business won't go under, or that the year we spent chasing the thing we long for will pay off.

And it doesn't always. Sometimes the hero just doesn't make it, and the story never gets told. You know that. I know that. What doesn't kill us gives us something to tell stories about. But when she does make it, and she takes hold of the Reward for which she struggled so hard, and takes the Road Back to the ordinary world, even still pursued by the villain, the enemy of our souls, or her own doubts, she experiences something of a rebirth, a Resurrection. She is changed, has faced her fears, her demons, and she has won, Returning Home, back to the tribe, the kingdom, the family, with the magic sword or elixir.

The dragons have only ever been metaphors for us, the swords now only symbols, but this pattern in one form or another has played out in a million eras on a million faces. And I think it's worth the time to write here and to think about, because I think it makes it easier when we wake up hearing that call to do something new, to venture past the threshold of the mundane (even if that's an everyday effort) to remember what's coming our way. It's easier to deal with the approach to our inmost cave, or deepest fears, when we can brace ourselves for it, and when we know that every artist through every age, whether their art was in raising monuments, raising money, or raising kids, has fought tooth and nail to get there, and that struggle has changed them before it's allowed them to go home and do it all again the next day.

Our own hero's journey, just as easily seen as the Artist's Journey or the Human's Journey, will both span our lives and repeat in smaller cycles, with each new book, each song we try to write, each canvas we fill, or each new initiative we begin when the words "what if..." wake us from our slumber and call us to the adventure. We will go through the same challenges, whether our conflict is with ourselves, the project we're working on, or something else. It won't make the struggle easier, but perhaps we'll have less fear, and blame ourselves less, when we know we're fighting on the same battleground. And it should make us nervous and raise red flags when the journey doesn't take us through those battlefields. If we haven't struggled with it, we will—or there's a good chance the work isn't worth the effort. I'm not saying it's always this way, I'm just saying that's the way it seems to be most of the time. Our art is only worth as much as it cost us.

Living a great story is much harder than watching a great story, but it's why we watch at all. The great movies steel our nerves and give us hope. They remind us that no story worth the telling, or the living, comes without conflict and struggle; they remind us that the necessary price we pay is transformation. The promise of any great story is that the hero never returns the same. Story is not about entertainment. It's about change, and it is change that makes us the artists—the humans—that we are and gives us the place from which we make our art and write our own stories; to live our lives with greater intention instead of allowing our stories merely to write themselves.

AN ACT OF CREATIVITY

This book began as a book about the creative process. And because the creative process is what it is, and part of that is it's reliable unpredictability, the book is becoming something else, something bigger, as I write it: a book about life as creative process. In part that has happened accidentally.

The more I've written—a chapter here or there—the more I've found unexpected connections between things I didn't initially see. The biggest connection has been the way the principles of an intentionally nurtured creative process mirror those of a life lived intentionally and creatively. So while I started out to write a book about the creative life, I've written something much more about the created life, which is fitting because the more I discuss creativity with others the more I see it touching every aspect of our lives, in every discipline, and if it can so permeate our lives I think it deserves a conversation that is larger than just how being creative relates to the life of the artist.

The creative process, in broad terms, is relatively predictable. We know something of how it works and we know *that* it works, in part because the human brain is just so truly good at what it does when it's all working as it should. But being able to rely on it doesn't remotely mean that we know exactly where it's going to take us. There are too many authors, musicians, or inventors who testify to the fact that the muse has dragged them into unexpected places, to ignore the serendipitous nature of the creative journey. If the creative process is predictable in broad strokes, it's wildly unpredictable in the details. But that doesn't mean we can't be as intentional about the life we're creating as we are about the work that fills our days.

Being intentional begins with a difficult question for most of us, difficult because we seem to have learned not to ask it. That question, asked in several different ways, is simply this: What do I want? What do I want to create? What kind of person do I want to become? What kind of people do I want to be surrounded by? What kind of legacy do I want to leave? And, conversely, what do I not want? For most of us it just seems easier to let life come as it does, to react to what comes, and one day find our lives have formed themselves into an ad hoc collection of all the decisions we chose not to make, all the ways we settled for things we never wanted. We find our house has been built of the flotsam and jetsam that's washed up on the beach and been banged together over the years, more from reaction to what's come our way than from an effort to build something specific.

I'm not sure if it's because we don't trust ourselves to be both ambitious and generous, but we've come to equate ambitious people with people who hunger for power. Ambition is a fuel and the machine it powers can be used for good or evil. But it's not the fault of ambition when people choose to aspire to less than noble things.

It takes great ambition to do the things of which Mother Teresa or Gandhi were capable. It takes focused intent to dedicate your days to perfecting a heart implant or the discovery of a cure for cancer, but those are not the only efforts to which ambition is nobly applied. It takes ambition to do your art, to write your book, to raise your children to be everything you hope for them. And yes, it takes ambition and some difficult honesty to admit that what you want is to make an astonishing amount of money in order to do astonishing things that cost money. Someone has to pay for cancer research. It's easy for artists to say they don't think about these things, but try being broke or on the edge of bankruptcy and you'll see that you think about money much, much more than you ever imagined.

Being hungry and dodging creditors as you pursue your art is not noble, nor is it likely (necessarily) to lead to great art. Of course, money is not the point here. Desire it or don't, but you can't ignore it because too many good, beautiful, world-changing things come at a cost and unless you find someone willing to cure cancer or teach your children by bartering for a chicken or a goat, cash will be preferred, because they too have bills to pay. If you want it, money or otherwise, it'll be easier to come by if you're honest and intentional about making it. Sure, people discover things by accident, but for the most part even those accidental discoveries were made while they were intentionally looking for *something*. Search for nothing and you're bound to find it. Strive for nothing, hope for nothing, and desire nothing, and there's a better chance than not that you'll get exactly what you strive for, hope for, and desire: nothing.

This is not the same sermon as the one that starts with "If you can dream it, you really can do it." A wonderful notion, but not one based in any reality I'm familiar with. I've failed at plenty of things I've been able to dream of. But I'm not sure I'd have known one way or the other for certain unless I tried. Anyone who hopes to spend any time doing anything creative will become more familiar than they'd like to be with the reality that this, whatever this is at the time, just might not work. But it sure as hell won't work if you don't try.

THIS MIGHT NOT WORK

I took a forced hiatus in 2011 from my work as a photographer for humanitarian organizations, the result of an accident in Italy that left me unable to walk. The last assignment I did, in the far reaches of northern Kenya among nomadic Rendille, Turkana, and Samburu tribes, changed my life.

As I write this chapter it's January 2013 and I'm on my way back to Kenya, my head full of ideas and the expectations I should know well enough not to have. I have all kinds of notions about what my work—my resulting photographs—will be like, which sits uneasily beside the knowledge that what I will accomplish, and what images I return with, will not be that. Whatever I create there will come from that heady, addictive mix of my own hopes for this work, and serendipity. Unforeseen, and uncontrollable, the days ahead will come without needing my permission but open to my collaboration; my receptivity and a hungry willingness to say Yes to what comes my way will take the place of these expectations very quickly. They always do.

On top of all that, and the way my own expectations seem to constantly be getting in the way of seeing things as they truly are, a couple days into this I'll learn again to be receptive to *what is* instead of try to force *what may never be*. It is these expectations that define what it will be for me to fail. So I'll be worried about that too, until, as I said, I adjust those expectations and redefine what it means to succeed. I fight this battle so often, it's astonishing I'm still surprised when it happens.

That said, I know all too well that part of the life creative, of doing what's not been done before and trying new ways of accomplishing the familiar, is the promise of failure. Maybe I should use the word "risk" instead of "promise," but that's unkindly optimistic. Failure in the creative life is not only a risk, a possibility to be avoided, but an eventuality to be embraced. Worrying we *might* fail leads to fear and paralysis; it leads to making "safe" decisions instead of the ones demanded by our art, our longings. Knowing failure is part of our process leads to new ideas, stronger work, and more honest questions that liberates us to peer, a little less frightened, into the unknown.

I think much of this fear of failure is a question of expectation and definition. If we define success in our creative efforts as "getting it right the first time," then failure is, as I said, a promise. The alternative is mediocrity, and I'll take failure on these terms any day over mediocrity and first-effort results. If, instead, we define failure in terms of risks untaken, questions unasked, or work untried, then we go into those risks, questions, and work knowing there's a good chance we'll fall down a few times before we find our stride. To use a metaphor from childhood, failure is not in falling off the bike, it's in not getting back on and learning to ride the damn thing. Falling is assumed. It's our best, and most faithful, teacher. That doesn't mean, of course, that it doesn't hurt like hell; our pride especially smarts from this.

But really, who the hell do we think we are that we should accomplish something new without first bumping around in the darkness a little? Arrogance and a teachable spirit are mutually exclusive; as much as we all wish we could experience mastery after reading a couple books, we'd be crazy to expect it.

The words "this might not work" are probably some of the healthiest in the lexicon of anyone who wants to live creatively. They indicate a certain humility and openness to what comes next. Whether that is failure or success very much depends on how you define it. "This won't work" is defeatist. "This probably won't work" is self-fulfilling. "Let's see what happens" is rife with possibility.

I was a guest lecturer at an arts school in Vancouver recently. I taught for a couple hours, by which I mean I talked for a couple hours in hopes that some of my rambling words would find purchase in their beautiful young minds. I wanted an honest conversation about creativity and fear, and knowing this would be difficult, was surprised when the discussion turned meaningfully candid. Several times the fear of failure came up.

"I'm afraid I'll fail and it'll be too hard." It's always hard, and always has been. The difficulty is the measure of its worth, and is proportionately offset by the joy of creation. If it's easy, find something better to dedicate your too-few days to.

"I'm afraid I'll fail and have to get a *real job*." That might happen too. Hell, I went bankrupt, but no real job, especially a temporary one while you get back on your feet, will stop you from doing that one creative thing you long to do. You can still paint, write, sculpt, and start your business. Your schedule might be different than you planned, but it always is.

"I'm afraid I'll fail and my work won't be received." It won't be, and if getting negative critical feedback on your work is, for you, a failure, then you most certainly will fail. And you will fail over and over—unless you change your definition. What about making work that pleases you, in the full knowledge that there are millions out there that won't like what you create? The Beatles did. So did Warhol, Picasso, Steve Jobs, every artist you've ever admired, and, God help us, there are people that don't like what Mother Teresa did either, and I'd call her life a work art if ever there was such a thing.

To be blunt (and this is directed at myself first): Suck it up, princess. The only failure is to not do. The real failure is to rob this world of the contribution only you can make, and to fail to make work that truly gives you that "this is what I was created to do" feeling that has no equal—not drugs, alcohol, shiny stuff, or a lover's kiss. Having children might rival it, but I'd argue that's an act of creation, and one of the most primal. To do otherwise is to have failed, to admit that the praise of others is more important than your own work. It's a betrayal of your own voice in favour of the voices of the critics, and there is nothing I can think of that will send the muse packing, or kill her outright, faster than this.

Other failures sound more legitimate than this. They aren't.

"I'm scared I'll fail and my work won't be what I hope it to be." It won't. Get okay with that now. It will be different. Sometimes it will be more than you ever imagined; it will surprise you to the depths of your being and the muse will whisper, "See? I told you so." Sometimes it will be less than you hoped and you'll learn something while the muse, still whispering, says, "One more time, this time with *feeling*." And you'll do it again. Have you ever noticed how some novelists or songwriters seem to tell the same story, in different ways, over their entire career? My favourite writer, Chaim Potok, did so by refining his story through different plots and characters until the day he died. He didn't repeat himself; he built on his previous work. He evolved, and changed, and so did his writing. Nothing is *perfect* the first time. Or ever. Nothing.

A friend of mine used to run the Canadian studio of a brilliant and well-known story factory. You've seen their movies. We spent a long Thanksgiving weekend away last year, camping in a Jeep on the west coast of British Columbia's Vancouver Island, talking long and late about creativity. There might have been wine. One of the long conversations we had that weekend was about the

Too Perfect Theory, here capitalized for emphasis, not because it's necessarily a real thing with a real name. But it should be. I once studied sleight of hand and the art, and artifice, of illusion. One of the notions that informed this art—and when done right, it is art—was the idea that an illusion could be *too* perfect. When the illusion was too perfect, the audience rescinded their willing suspension of disbelief. In fact the most sustained moments of wonder I have ever experienced have occurred during Cirque du Soleil shows, their wires visible for all to see, but my wonder at their floating in air so much greater. And my friend echoed this. In the world of animation, anything too perfect was disbelieved. Why? The real world doesn't work like this. We find beauty, for example, not in perfect symmetry, but *near* symmetry. So not only is *nothing* perfect, there's little reason to aim at it. Perfection, so free of what it means to be human, resonates with few of us, and the things that do resonate as *perfect* are imperfectly so.

Failure? It's a question of definition, but it's going to happen, and it's going to take us, kicking and screaming, no doubt, and with broken bones and bruised egos, to better work. It will, to take us back to the idea that creating the artist is the first order of business, make us better, more human, creators. It'll make us happier too. Not to get too

Zen about it, but if it's true that *what's in the way is the way,* then accepting the essential failures is a beautiful part of, and not separate from, the creative life.

The only failure is not bouncing back, not learning from the thing. And I don't mean necessarily the big stuff. I mean the song that you've been pouring your heart into that just didn't land with the audience the way you'd hoped, or the exhibit of photographs that fell flat, or whatever creative project you took a risk on only to find it taking a turn you didn't expect. Expectations are a dangerous thing, and if we can allow our creativity to take us on an adventure (the definition of which includes detours and the shuttling of plans to the wayside), we're likely to find that those unexpected roadblocks, the ones that looked so much like failure when we were approaching them, look in hindsight like course corrections. Painful course corrections, if we're honest, but how many of us really learn the most valuable lessons the easy way? We label things as failures when our view is too short-sighted to see the whole picture.

You won't hear applause at every practice, nor get kudos and positive reviews on your crappy first drafts. Those are places we allow ourselves to fail safely, privately, and that's the only difference. You don't get to do all your failing in some dark corner, far from the world's eye. And when you do fail, assuming you get up and try again, it is only your pride that gets hurt, not your art. When you feel you've failed and never find the courage or the will to get up again, then it is your art that gets hurt at the expense of your pride, and that's a high price to pay for something so naturally part of the creative process as failure.

Failure is the testing of ideas that have yet to find their best expression. Buckminster Fuller said, "There is no such thing as a failed experiment, only experiments with unexpected outcomes." Miles Davis said, "Do not fear mistakes; there are none," which I take to mean that while not everything we do has an intended outcome, if it does not stop us and it gets us to an unexpected place of creativity, it is not to be feared. It still comes back to a fear of the unknown, which I believe we can learn to accept and embrace if we hold on to things a little less tightly.

CHOOSING YOUR RISK

There are no guarantees as we head into the unknown. There can't be.

If you want to create something new, whether that's a novel or an unconventional life, there is no getting around the risk, and anyone anywhere that sells you something using the word "risk-free" is lying. There is always, always, a risk. Risk of doing. Risk of not doing. The question is not whether or not there is a risk, but what the risks are. A friend of mine has always been risk-averse. Now that I think about it, many of my friends have been. They don't travel. They don't quit the jobs that are quietly killing their souls. They don't step out and follow their dreams of becoming a musician, or novelist, or that guy that sells his house to sail around the world. It's too risky.

Too risky? Life is risky! And lest you think selling your house and sailing around the world is risky, how about the risk of not doing the one thing you've dreamed of since you were seven years old reading *The Kon-Tiki Expedition*, and dying with regrets instead? How about the risk of teaching your children that following your dreams is less important than remaining safe, going to college, and dying unfulfilled? Sure, there's a risk in taking your kids out of school and teaching them yourself while you travel. But is it greater or worse than the risk of leaving them in a class of 30 other students, with an exhausted teacher, surrounded by homogeny? That's for you to decide.

The chronically employed see a life of self-employment and entrepreneurialism as too risky, not safe enough. Never having had a real job as an adult, I've seen friends lose their jobs, betrayed by the safety they felt they had by betting on the nameless, faceless man running a corporation created to make money, not to care for them, and I see chronic employment as too great a risk for me. I'd rather have the freedom to change with the economy, a freedom most companies don't have, and by the time they change course it's too late: time for layoffs. I'd rather bet on my own ability to learn, to succeed, and yes—to fail and bounce back. I control the amount of my bet, and I know what I'm betting on. I can't avoid risk, but I can intentionally choose the risks that come with the life I desire.

It's risky to leave the job you hate. It's also risky, and at so high a cost, to stay there at the expense of sanity and soul. How many nights can you lie in bed staring at the ceiling, replaying conflicts and demeaning conversations with the boss? How long is your life that you can wait another five years before you cut your hours back so you can invest them instead in your own business?

It's risky, too, to write a book, cut an album, or put your things into the back of your truck and set off across the continent, which I did in 2010, unable to reconcile myself any longer to taking the risk of it never happening. So I sold every piece of furniture I had, relinquished my lease on a nice apartment, and piled my cameras, laptops, and clothing into a 1993 Land Rover Defender with a rooftop tent, and set off down the west coast from Vancouver to take a year and circle the U.S. and Canada.

I wanted to experience things I would never experience at home, find some new stories, and meet new people. I wanted to camp out in places like Monument Valley and the coast of Texas along the Gulf of Mexico. So many people told me they wished they could do what I did, and said so with such longing, never seeing that they could do it as readily as I could, but would have to make similar choices, taking similar risks, as I did. In the end I suffered no major breakdown, met no horrible end in some dark corner of the continent, and didn't get sick. Nothing I was warned about happened.

Instead I was in Italy, the Land Rover parked in Atlanta for a month, when I fell off a 30-foot wall onto concrete below. I landed, like a cat—or a ninja, if you prefer—on my feet. And then I crumpled, which is what you do when you've fallen that far and landed on your feet, shattering both of them and cracking your pelvis. I ended up in the hospital in Pisa after a dramatic rescue and an ambulance ride, where I spent four days before my medical evacuation could take place and I was finally (and very heavily) sedated and put on a medical jet home to Canada.

After 40 days and nights, and surgery on my feet, I was sent home, able only to crawl, to recover at my family home, learn to walk again, and finish my fourth book. A hundred warnings about the risks of taking a journey on which I was happier than I'd been in years, and not a soul told me to be careful in Tuscany.

You just can't know. I've done assignments for clients in places like Haiti, Bosnia, Democratic Republic of Congo, Ethiopia, and El Salvador. All places the U.S. State Department counselled its citizens not to visit. I'm Canadian, so I guess I get a free pass. And in all of them I was fine. I go to Tuscany to teach photography and I'm painfully broken. I will never walk the same again. What arrogance to assume we can know the true cost of anything we do. What loss to put aside the things we long—with all our hearts—to do, fearful of the risks, as if we have the first idea what those risks might even be.

The imagined risks may never happen. And we're sidelined by the ones we never in a million years might have anticipated. I'd rather take the risk of being broken all over again than to sit safely at home only to be diagnosed, far too early in life, with cancer and be surrounded in my final days with family, friends, and bitter regret.

It's not about avoiding risk. It never is. Because the risk is always there and always truly unknown. There are no safe bets. What there is, and always has been, is choice in the face of the unknown. You follow your heart and the best wisdom you can find in the light available to you, and then you choose. Intentionally, wholeheartedly, and knowing there will be fears and doubts, and parts of it will be scary as all hell at times. To do otherwise—to play it safe—is delusional, because safety is an illusion. "I can't risk it" is the way we talk when we've abdicated responsibility for making our lives extraordinary, a thing we can create intentionally. It's what we say when we lack the balls to say we choose to do A over B, knowing there are risks inherent in both. Life, and art, is about choosing.

The best things in life are discovered after walking through gates clearly warning of so-called risks ahead. Love. Art. Investments. Adventure. Upon seeing those signs, it's harder to turn back, when you know that the moment you turn your back on those risks, you see signs warning of the risks of walking away. And you don't always know. And you won't always make the right choice. But you have one life to live and one chance to live it to its fullest, and to teach your children and friends to do the same. Don't you dare wait until it's crystal clear; it will never be. Nor should you choose to ignore your heart for the sake of what others expect or because it's a little easier to do so. It will kill your soul. The soil in which you plant your seeds will be mediocre, and the fruit will be bland to others and bitter to you.

LIVING ABOVE THE 45

My friend Dylan is a gifted animator. He's extremely talented in that Renaissance Man kind of way that would make you want to hate him if he weren't so damn likeable. A few years ago he was speaking at a creative event in Vancouver and I popped in to see his talk. He talked about living past our comfort zone and it kept me awake and thinking, all the way to Bosnia where I was heading to photograph for a client in the rural areas around Sarajevo.

The thing about Dylan's talk, the thing that shook me up, was that I thought I knew better. I thought I was living the life he was advocating. Hell, I was about to sell everything I owned and spend a year driving around North America in my 20-year-old Land Rover. If anyone was living above the 45, and I'll explain that in a moment, it was me. Turns out you have to put yourself there every day, because the 45 is relative to who we are, and that keeps changing.

Dylan described "Living Above the 45" in the following way. Imagine your life on a graph. On one axis you've got the opportunities and challenges we undertake or submit ourselves to. On the other axis are your abilities and comfort level—essentially your perceived ability to handle the opportunities and challenges. When the two are equal to each other, the line bisecting the graph is at 45 degrees. Everything at that line on the 45 is in balance. More bluntly, it represents stagnation, because growth only happens when the opportunities we create or seize outpace our talent, ability, or comfort. To further abuse an already ill-fitting metaphor, biting off more than we feel we can chew is the only way to grow in our capacity to chew more.

It's above the 45, and only above the 45, where growth happens and where we stop repeating ourselves and create something beautiful, important, or good. When creatives and artists get stalled on the idea of making money with every project and paying the rent, they abandon the muse, because the muse doesn't give a hot damn whether you make money. She cares about making something beautiful and honest, about creating something that will outlast us. And while there are too many people that will put down a few bucks for something mediocre, there are as many people willing to put down more for something amazing, something beautiful, something that took risk and honesty to create. So take the risk and trust that it'll pay off.

It's when we live above the 45 that we begin creating things for the very reasons for which we stayed below the 45. It applies to more than just creation in the artistic sense. It applies to raising children, growing a business, and keeping the flames of a relationship lit and raging. Life is lived most vitally above the 45. To hell with balance. Leave that to the mediocre, the uninspired, and the uninspiring.

At the risk of flirting with presumptuous inspirational nonsense, are you living consistently above the 45? Are you one step ahead of your fear or has it been a while since you even considered its presence? Are you growing or stagnating? Moving forward or back? I ask because my own answer is not always Yes.

On the day I heard Dylan talk I was, as I said, heading out on assignment to Bosnia. I was packing up my home to live the life nomadic when I returned. To all appearances I was above the 45, but in significant ways I wasn't. I wasn't pushing my craft. I wasn't leaning into the fear. Not the way I thought I was, anyway. What looked difficult and fearless to others was comfortable to me. What is above and below that 45-degree line is relative to each of us. And it's ever-changing, which is why it's so easy to wake one morning to find ourselves stagnant. We didn't move an inch, but the line shifts, slowly, ever higher, and one day we realize we've been living below the line instead of above it.

The magic rarely happens within our comfort zone, but outside it, on the ragged, scary edge, where we have to fight like hell to keep from drowning in the unknown. This is where most of us create our best stuff, have our most adventurous thoughts, and feel the most alive. No one lives above the 45 by accident. You wake up every day and decide, not to wait for inspiration, but to work, to do the best work of your life, even your life's work. You don't sit around waiting for your real life to begin, because those that do will find it never comes, or some other unexpected horror comes first to wake us and our waited-for dreams slip away.

Now is the time to feed your hunger for freedom, for beauty, for meaningful work. It's not, Seneca said, that we live for too short a time, but that we waste so much of it.

PRETENDING TO BE BRAVE

A handful of years ago you couldn't swing a dead cat, forgive the expression, without hitting a kid wearing a t-shirt that read, optimistically, NO FEAR. You don't see a lot of those shirts anymore, probably because the people wearing them died doing things their fear might otherwise have prevented or, more likely, they realized the propaganda didn't live up to the reality. Ironically, I suspect more people wore the shirt out of a desire to fit in, a backhanded way of saying they were *afraid* they wouldn't. No fear, indeed.

Fear has a place in our lives, much the same as pain. Put your hand in the fire as a child, you get burned. Unless you're a very slow learner, you won't do that many more times before it occurs to you: I should stop doing that. Pain is a good teacher, fear makes the lesson stick; it stops us from getting burned again.

As we grow up, the same thing happens over and over again with different flames. In second grade we sing a song for show-and-tell and are rewarded with ridicule. It'll be a long time before we sing in public again. We venture to give an opinion in class and are called out for being stupid. We take our first risk in love and have our heart broken. We try a game we've never played, fail the first time in front of others, and discover what our fear will tell us for the rest of our lives: it's safer not to try.

Fear wants nothing more for us than our own safety, and if safe is all you long for, then your fears will serve you well. But I know very few people who—once safe—long to remain there. Stay there long enough and paralysis sets in.

Because the creative life is lived, necessarily, on the edges of "I haven't done this before," it is lived in risk. Step outside the safety of the rules, into the beautiful anarchy of creativity, invention, and expression, and we step, with both feet, into the unknown. We step into the unfamiliar and our fears rush in with panicked voices of warning. Stop! Remember the last time you did that? Rejection! Shame! Failure!

The greatest obstacle to the creative life is not fear itself, but what we do with it. I know no one, creative or otherwise, who lives without fear. The challenge is not to find a place free from fear, but a way to put fear in its proper place. For some of us that means first acknowledging the fear and calling it out of the shadows.

When I was 24 I hastily married, one-half of a desperate union of two ill-fitting people trying earnestly to be years more mature than we were. Six years later we were divorcing, and the friction and hurt had made me, and probably both of us, very angry. A friend at the time suggested anger was connected to fear and suggested I make a list of my fears and see if any of them were really as bad as they (my fears) kept promising, usually late at night when my world seemed to be collapsing on me with greater consequence than it did in the daytime. I don't know if he had in mind an actual list, but I grabbed a pad of paper, a pen, and a cup of coffee.

The coffee was cold by the time my list, a couple pages long, was complete. It could have been shorter but I've never been known for brevity. Just seeing my fears called by name was helpful. But more helpful was the moment I pulled them, one by one, into the light to size them up. In each case I discovered their voices more frightening than the thing they represented. Each of them preyed on my past in some way, and found their power in what I did not know. I was losing my marriage. What else would I lose? My friends? The respect of my family? My financial stability? I had no idea, and it was not knowing that scared me so much.

Fear isn't easily turned back, but it loses its power quickly when you shine a light into the dark areas from which it whispers. Leave it whispering in the shadows and it grows, in part because it's always rooted in some truth, some actual possibility. We've been hurt before, and we remember the very real sting of the pain. Our fear only reminds us of that pain and points out the possibility of being burned by the same flame again. It's because these fears find their fulcrum on a small corner of truth that they get such leverage and are so hard to ignore. If they were complete bullshit, we'd ignore them outright. But they aren't. They might be right. What if…?

After I made my list I looked at each fear. I asked questions like: Really? So what? What's the alternative? In each case the fear became manageable, helped by knowing none of this would actually kill me, and that I truly had no choice but to move forward, at least not if I wanted to survive emotionally. And where the fears still loomed, I discovered a courage I didn't know I had. Yes, I might lose friends, but I'd keep those who mattered. Yes, I might have a long financial recovery ahead, but I wouldn't lose the only real asset with which I made my living: my creativity. It was in that single word, "but," that I found my courage.

Whatever our fears, I know no one who has found a way to live without them. Courage is not an absence of fear, but an act of the will to move forward in the presence of fear. Fear whispers, "You might…" Courage rebuffs it with, "Sure, but…." To seek a fearless life is not the same as seeking a life of courage.

If we're talking about story, which is about nothing if not life, no one gives a damn about fearlessness. Very few great stories move forward with a fearless hero. Why would they? Not only is there nothing to gain from a hero without fear, there's not a single one of us out here in the real world who resonates with that. Instead, we resonate with courage and the very real struggle to find it. There's a great line in the movie *The Ghost and the Darkness*, which is on my mind now because at this moment I'm sitting in a tent in Tsavo, Kenya, where the story about the infamous man-eating lions took place. Michael Douglas's character, the hunter Remington, on the eve of the hunt in which they hope to kill the lions, walks off to join the Maasai warriors dancing around the fire, telling his friends, "I'm going to join them now, maybe try to convince each other we're still brave." One of the men says, "I wouldn't have thought bravery would be a problem for you." He replies, "Well, you hope each time it won't be…but you never know."

The world resonates with courage, and the will to press on, not with fearlessness. Because we resonate with it so much we've come to glorify it, making it something we feel somewhat self-conscious about attributing to ourselves, like humility. It's the same with the word "Art." Ask an artist if they have courage and they'll say, "No. And I'm not really an artist." But they do. And they are. We've made more of it than we should, so it feels a little unattainable. Call it determination if you feel more comfortable being determined. Call it stubborn if you're more the self-deprecating type. Call it whatever you want. What matters is that you acknowledge your fears, hear them out, and when they point to some painful possibility, you harness your will and move forward, regardless, into the unknown, which is the only place in which we do our work.

Fear is speculative. Nothing more. It uses the word "might" a lot. As in, "You might die a horrible death." Fear is a little melodramatic and is very poor at looking forward with anything but guesses. If it did look forward with any clarity it would also see regret for the things it holds us back from: things untried, work unaccomplished, words unsaid. And we would, I think, fear those much more. We put off writing a book, starting a new business, or singing in front of others because we fear the same sting of rejection or failure we've felt before. Fear holds us back. Fear does not pull us forward with the same strength when there's as much reason to regret not doing those same things. What of the fear of regret? Regret from missed opportunity, missed glory, missed chances to make of our lives, even our smallest moments, something astonishing, important, or helpful?

Fear is better at looking back at past hurts. They're over. Done. They aren't coming back except when we bid them to. If you want a voice that looks forward, I think you'll only hear it in the brave whispering of courage when it says, "Yes, but...."

If you want to make fear a more positive force, then words credited to Lao Tse Tung might be helpful: "What's in the way, is the way." Steven Pressfield, the author of *The War of Art*, less obliquely says our fear points us towards the very thing we ought to be doing. The greater our fears over some new venture, the more urgently we should be walking in that very direction. "Yes, I know, but I'm scared..." Exactly. Do it anyway. Rewards are greatest where the risk is greatest. If you can't be brave, pretend you are. No one's looking. We're all too busy pretending we're brave ourselves.

LISTENING TO VOICES

We all hear voices. We're surrounded by them, and as social media becomes more a part of our lives, they're becoming more numerous, less personal, and much, much louder. Besides the constant squeaking of media, there are voices from the past, from peers and colleagues, from loved ones and that place inside, out of which pours an endless stream of conflicting voices, alternately cheering us on and pulling us back. Hearing voices, barring some psychotic episode, is not the problem; it's choosing which ones to listen to and which ones to ignore.

It would be so much easier if we could simply box these voices into categories, embracing the good voices, ignoring the bad. But life isn't often so easily dichotomized. In fact, a constant stream of encouragement from the wrong sources can be as hindering to us as giving no heed to well-meaning but critical voices in our lives. Both can keep us well and truly anchored in mediocrity.

My mother told me, from as far back as my earliest memories can take me, that I can do anything I want to. She encouraged me to let that belief inform my actions, and I still believe, with some well-founded exceptions, that I can in fact do anything I want to. But when my hopes, brief as they were, to become a doctor collided with a complete inability to make sense of math, she was equally encouraging: I could do *anything else* I wanted. By that time I'd lost the desire to go into medicine, in part because I didn't enjoy anything associated with that path: not biology, not chemistry. What I loved was art and language, and anything that allowed me to think outside the box in a way that math didn't seem to allow.

Our parents' desires for us can as easily hold us back. Without seeing that my gifts and aptitudes lay here instead of there, my mother might have insisted I keep at it, told me not to "waste my time" on my photography or drawing, or whatever creative outlet was keeping my attention at the time.

The words "Keep at it!" can push us forward or hold us back. I think the same is true of more critical voices, like the teacher, father, or coach for whom no performance is good enough. As a child it's hard to filter these voices out so rationally, but as adults hearing those voices now, they can either help us aim higher or discourage us to the point of resignation. It is not the voices that mean a damn thing; it's our reaction to them. It's not what people say; it's what we hear.

"What did he mean by that?" is a great question when we hear those voices. But perhaps more important is, "What do I do with that?" In the case of a friend who constantly praises your work, the intention is clear, but if you're honest about wanting to be better at what you do, you need to ask if that voice is really helpful. Perhaps an enthusiastic friend will make you feel better about your work when what you need is someone who's able to give you actual feedback. In other words, listen to Mom when she puts your art on the fridge and tells you it's the most beautiful thing she's ever seen, but don't let that stop you from hearing your art teacher when he tells you it's time to move past the stick figures. One voice tells you to keep doing it, the other tells you to keep doing it better.

So what do we do when the voices aren't so kind? Ignore them! To hell with the naysayers! Not so fast. Even if it were possible to so easily ignore the critics, I think we need to hear what they say before we so easily dismiss them. Even jerks and morons have a point once in a while.

Each time one of my books has come out, I've waited nervously to read the Amazon reviews that eventually get written. Most of them are great, written by very obviously kind and intelligent people with great taste. Those are the positive reviews. A very few of them are less positive. One guy called me "fat, bald, and ugly," to which I took great exception, because I'm really not that bald yet. The personal attacks are easy to dismiss. But to receive the praise of strangers as unthinkingly as I dismiss their criticism is, I think, a touch on the hypocritical side. Or at very least it's missing a chance to learn something.

Once the book's written, it's true that I can't exactly make the changes some of these critical voices call for. But if over the course of several books these critical voices (the sane ones, at any rate) all point to a similar weakness in my writing, then they've given me something the cheerleaders have not: a chance to learn. If what you want is to be praised, then read the good and leave the bad. If what you want is to beat yourself up, then do the reverse. But if you want to learn, give the voices a chance, and sift the helpful from the harmful before you take them too personally.

On the extreme ends, there will always be sycophants and assholes. I suggest we ignore them both, but the moderate voices should be given a hearing. Unless they're all sycophants and assholes, in which case you're in trouble.

Cheerleaders have one job, and critics have another. It's wise to know which are which. But in the end, there is one voice that you must listen to above all others, and that is your own. The only problem is this: our own voice can be as negatively critical, or as blindly positive, as any voice you'll hear outside your own head. Still....

Sylvia Plath is quoted as saying the worst enemy of creativity is self-doubt. More than likely a result of hearing so many voices for so long, self-doubt paralyzes like little else. It's fear in a different guise, and I don't know of a way to get rid of it. We could spend a lifetime trying to unravel the voices that led us to this place, but who's got the time or the emotional resources to do so? We can do all the self-affirmations we want, and for some that might help, but I've tried, and while one part of me is saying, "You can do this!" the other part of me, the one that's supposed to be listening to the affirmation, is saying, "I doubt it." So when the emotional impasse has me completely exhausted, I ask myself a better question than "What can you do?" I ask, "What do you *want* to do?" Or on better days, "What *will* you do?" And then I try.

And maybe I'm right—maybe I can't do it. But then maybe I can and it won't turn out the way I expect anyway. Maybe people will love what I create, but it will fall short of my own hopes. Or maybe my own hopes will be met and the critics will abhor it. The outcome is a guess, at best. What is guaranteed is that if I never do the work, I'll never have a chance to enjoy all the things that process brings to me. The photograph I make might thrill me, or it might disappoint, but the joy of holding the camera, or learning something new, or allowing the disappointing image to lead me to a better one will never be mine if I allow my doubts to stop me from trying.

The difference between someone who serves their muse and their work and someone who serves their ego is that the one is willing to listen to self-doubt and move forward despite it, and the other stops short. One will do everything to protect the work; the other will do anything to protect themselves. And the life creative is never—ever—lived without frightening, intoxicating risk.

We all wrestle with self-doubt. It's a natural companion to the humility that keeps us teachable and honest. It's when self-doubt spirals downward into self-pity that things begin to go dangerously off the rails for the creative spirit. Self-pity isn't humility: it's indulgent and arrogant. I have seen it enough in myself to know its toxic effect.

Self-pity gets its momentum from the assumption that all this—life and art—should be easier for us than it is, that creating anything of any value should come without effort or cost. It comes from the assumption that our own creative process should come without the same struggle faced by every other person who tried to live creatively and make something the world's never seen before. We should get it right the first time. Why? No one else does it that way. What makes us so special? We've paid our dues longer? We've got fancy business cards with the word "professional" on them?

At the risk of being too direct, the muse doesn't give a damn about anything but your willingness to feed her and honour the process with your sweat. Life is not easy, or even fair. The muse doesn't stick around longer or give you inspiration that burns with a brighter flame because of past success or how much you had to give up to get to this point. She cares about one thing alone: the art you make with your life. She doesn't care how bruised you become, how much sleep you have to lose, or how much criticism you have to bear in order to get there.

Maybe I'm being too harsh; it could be that some of us just don't know that creation comes out of chaos, and with tears, frustration, and too many do-overs. It could be that our self-pity comes not from pride but from ignorance. We just didn't know. Everyone else makes it look so fucking easy. I get that. But now you know.

Seeing only the final work of the so-called pros in any field of endeavour can leave us feeling inadequate. Reading the best-seller and not seeing the years of rewriting and the piles of rejection letters beside that now-empty bottle of gin makes it seem easy. We seldom see the final painting with any clue as to the frustration, boredom, and hours spent scraping the canvas and beginning again that it took to get there. We're presented with a final product so beautiful that it retains no trace of the difficult process. It's little wonder we spend too much time in the emotional darkness of self-pity, preferring the voice of sympathy to the voice of the muse.

It's important to understand we're not alone. It's important to know that what we do when we conjure something from nothing is hard for us all. None of us has a sterile process, and I suspect if we do, we're not creating much of value. A sterile process creates sterile art, which moves no one. It's the difficulty of the process itself that makes us who we are, and from which flows our best work. It's that struggle that give us the best chance of getting past the obvious, the cliché, and the done-before, and into more honest work. Among the voices to which we need to listen are those of other artists. Not only the voices of triumph that come when some created thing is born, finally, but also the curses and mutterings and frustrated sighs that come during the labour. Imagine the terror of a new mother who has no idea that childbirth is going to take so long, and hurt so much, and that this is the way it's always been. It hurts no less when we know what's coming, when we know that this is the way of things, but it takes away some of the fear.

There is a difference between pain and harm and I think that being unable to see that difference sits at the bottom of why we fear some things so unnecessarily, and allow that pain to paralyze us. We fear the pain of losing something we love, of humiliation, of failure, and all those million other things that jolt us awake at night, because not only does it hurt, and hurt is unpleasant, but we've come to know hurt and harm as the same thing, which it is not.

Lying on my massage therapist's table with tears pooling on my pillow as she strips apart layers of scar tissue in my legs, I feel pain, but no fear. Fear is absent because I trust my therapist and I know that the pain is temporary and leading me somewhere better. With every visit I leave her office straighter, and walk with less pain; I know it will be the same this time, even if the sensations in my legs at this very moment are sharply painful. I think the key word there is "trust." I trust her to heal, and not to harm.

But when we equate hurt with harm, and where trust is absent, we fear. Our survival instinct kicks in, and it's either fight or flight. A lifetime of equating hurt with harm, and responding accordingly, has created well-worn pathways in our brains, pathways that have to be consciously re-mapped if we're ever to see hurt and harm as different things and take Nietzsche at his word when he tells us, "That which doesn't kill us makes us stronger."

For most of us, it is not the pain that hurts us. It is the fear that arises from that pain, and the ways in which we live from that fear. Our hearts are broken, we feel great pain, and the first wall around our heart goes up almost overnight unless we make a conscious decision to leave the battlements unbuilt. We try, we fail, and we do not try again for fear of another failure. And in not trying again we lose a chance to succeed at the thing that—like most things in life—doesn't come to anyone on the first or second try. If we're not careful, our responses to the things in life that hurt us can cause a wound far more harmful than the initial hurt ever could. If we're to fear anything, it should be that.

Art is hard. So is life. I think one of the reasons it's so hard is that making art, or creating anything of worth in life, reveals who we are. It tells us about ourselves. Much as we long for our work to be a stained-glass window, it proves just as often to be a mirror, and it's unflinching. That's hard. It offers all kinds of reasons for fear, for procrastination. But there is also the knowledge that our work reveals who we are to others. Hard as it is, vulnerability is powerful. It changes our relationships and gives depth to anything we touch, and our art will be best where we allow ourselves the trauma of transparency. The sooner we care more for what we create than for the opinions of others, the sooner our art will become bigger than us.

Back to the voices. As Shakespeare's play *King Lear* comes to an end, the next to final words are from Edgar. Almost everyone else is dead, a result of all the lies and insincere words spoken to please the ego of a king, and he says: "The weight of this sad time we must obey: speak what we feel, not what we ought to say." Not one to miss a chance at pointing out the moral of the story, Shakespeare is urging us to speak, not from obligation, but from our hearts, and his final curtain falls on a stage full of corpses to underline the point.

As creatives, if not simply as human beings, among the voices we fail to listen to are our own. And when we do, we often tell ourselves the things we feel we *should* say, and not what we long to say. It might just be time to sit down for an hour, or a day's retreat somewhere, to pour yourself a cup of coffee or maybe a stiff drink, and be honest with yourself. No one's listening, so please, get it out.

Get what out? I have no idea. That's up to you. For me it was an admission of all the things I truly wanted, but for one reason or another was ashamed to admit I wanted. It was an admission that I *wanted* to write a best-selling book. I *wanted* to make a difference with my work. I *wanted* to travel the world. I *wanted* to make the work I *wanted* to make and not the work a client asked me to make. And yes, I *wanted* to make money doing what I loved. In smaller ways, they are admissions of what I want from my creative process—and allowing that to channel my work according to my desires and curiosities instead of allowing my marketing niche to become a creative rut. So many of us have been taught not to speak like this, not even to think honestly like this. Just who does he think he is, anyway? What makes him so special? Like crabs in a bucket, we tend to pull the ambitious ones back in.

This book comes from my honest search for a life that is genuine, passionate, generous, and full of the things, activities, and relationships I want. My own list of desires and hopes and ambitions for my life and work will be different than yours, as will my skills, talents, and life experiences. So the way in which I live my life, and the path I bash out of the jungle to do so, will be different than anyone else's. It begins with being honest about what I want.

Whether you're Mother Teresa or a Machiavellian opportunist is not my concern; the world is full of people who long for good things, and those who seem bent on making it to the top at the expense of others. It is what you long for and what price you're willing to pay, or allow others to pay, to get there for which others might have good cause to judge you, not that you hunger deeply. That you long for something more is the fire that will fuel your efforts to find it; denying that longing will only dilute the fuel. Deny it long enough and you'll find the fuel has no capacity to ignite. Or else it will have completely evaporated. The desire will still be there, but your strength to do anything about it will have long dried up.

To hear your own voice—your longing, your ambition— you must first give it permission to speak. I think this permission comes to us naturally, but I suspect it's been gently (and sometimes not so) beaten out of us. Children can seem surprisingly abrupt to adults; they speak their minds, and give voice to their desires and opinions, until they get taught that it's better to be polite than honest. We learn early to play from what Ralph Waldo Emerson called "the rulebook of nice." That rulebook, unwritten and unspoken, but known well by those of us that aren't simply sociopathic or completely oblivious to others, has one purpose: to stop the boat from rocking. The most obvious side effect is the silence of our voices, especially those that dissent.

And that's the problem. We've learned to keep our mouths shut on anything that takes us away from normal, or the status quo. We avoid rocking the boat at all costs. And if we keep those mouths shut long enough they either lose their power to speak at all, or they can remain shut no longer and when they finally open they do so with such unrestrained power that they harm more than they help. We don't need more voices that parrot the things already said, or that reinforce the mantra, "But we've always done it this way." We need voices willing to ask, "What if?" We need voices, both as a society and as individual human beings, to dissent to what is not working, to refuse to be part of the suffocating homogeny. And, to be more positive, we need voices unashamed to say, "I love you," or point out what is right, and beautiful, about the people around us.

That's the voice of anarchy I'm arguing for: the voice that refuses to sing from the rulebook of nice and instead chooses words that are more honest. In so doing we wind up speaking something better than "nice." We speak words that are kind, because if our words aren't honest, then they really aren't nice at all. I'm not talking about being "brutally honest." I don't believe in brutality, honest or otherwise. One of the kindest things we can do for those around us is to live honestly, free from hypocrisy, and give others the permission to do the same. From that place of honest, respectful existence is where it becomes possible to live the lives most closely aligned with our ambitions and talents. It's there that freedom and contentment and gratitude find their best voice and loudest volume.

I know I'm repeating myself, but: what do you want? What do you truly want? Getting what you want may seem impossible. It might, in fact, be impossible. The way may not seem obvious right now. But how can we know without first admitting our hunger? This might be one of the hardest things we ever do; for some it's opening a box we've fought hard to keep closed. Let this one out and you may never get the box closed again. You might fight for the rest of your life to meet those longings, fulfill those desires, realize those ambitions. God knows there are voices enough telling us we can't, or we shouldn't: the price is too high. The failure too humiliating. And what about the kids?

What about the kids? I'm not a parent, but there has to be some value in children growing up with parents that keep telling them to live their dreams and are, themselves, not too scared to live their own. Too risk averse. Or worse, keep using the kids to hold them back. No one is suggesting you leave home and abandon the kids to pursue your dream of being a professional NASCAR driver. Just admit that the dreams are there. Listen to that voice. Maybe, for now, it's enough that you share that dream with your kids, and take them go-karting on weekends. We rarely have any idea where things will lead, what possibilities will open up to us. But if you keep that voice muted, refuse to hear it, then the possibilities remain closed.

All of us hear voices, and those voices fall anywhere on the spectrum from dark and harmful to being full of light and love. Hearing those voices is not the problem; the problem is listening to them without sifting the truth from the lies, and listening to them at such volume that we drown out the voice most important in creating something beautiful of our lives: our own.

INSPIRATION

Inspiration comes from work, or so it is said. But what if we've got this whole "inspiration" metaphor wrong? If there's something to the language of this, then the word "inspire" means to breathe in. A deep breath is invigorating, to be sure, but I don't know anyone who takes one deep breath, then goes to work while holding it. "I was inspired!" we say. Great. But you're turning blue. Breathe out.

Creative people look for inspiration like it's the Holy Grail. It is not. It's a practice, and that practice is directly tied to work. If an inflow of ideas and thoughts and what-ifs are our act of breathing in, it is at work we breathe out, clear the lungs, and make the repetition of the process possible.

The most creative people exhibit this ebb and flow of constantly inhaling and exhaling. They put their thoughts into sketchbooks, they make photographs with their cameras, they sit down and write, or sit at the wheel to throw a pot, understanding that one thing leads to another. It is not so simple as waiting for a great idea to come out of the blue, the gift of the muse we call "inspiration." It's no one's job but yours to breathe—not the muses, angels, or anyone else. Only you can do that.

I think there's something good about this idea of our ideas coming from a source beyond us. I think it shows a certain humility. But it comes from a time when we credited the gods with everything. On one hand, it allows us to avoid hubris, but on the other it allows us the luxury of avoiding responsibility for our own creativity. After all, if the gods don't deliver, it's hardly my fault.

Our brains are astonishing organs. They do things we don't yet remotely understand, though we're coming to that knowledge, and the more we know, the more amazing it is. Steve Jobs said that creativity is merely connecting the dots, which is a good picture of what the brain does. Our thoughts and ideas are the connections between dots in our brain. Those dots are there because we've collected them in a lifetime of experiences, and the more dots we collect, the more connections are possible. That collection of experiences is our inspiration, our breathing in. Playing with those connections—with paint, words, clay, programming languages, wood, or whatever medium we prefer—is the way we exhale. In and out. Repeat.

It's a cycle. We may not find genius in each cycle; it might take many cycles before the best of our ideas are revealed; A+B might lead to C, and C+D might lead to E. But you might need a good deal more of the alphabet before you've got the raw materials for the poem within you. And you might not know the poem is even there until you've unearthed all the letters, played with the words, and discovered it there. And when you do, it won't be a bolt out of the blue, a sudden gift of the gods, but a result of that astonishing brain making unforeseen connections out of the dots you've worked so hard to connect. That doesn't make it any less miraculous, and you can thank Whomever you like for the gift of that brain, but had you not fed that brain by breathing—both physically and figuratively—you'd still be waiting. Or you'd pass out.

If creativity is, in part, about connecting dots, then the more divergent (or unlikely) those dots are, the better, and it is the daily task of the creative to be curious and collect dots. The most creative people I know fill their brains, their idea factories, with as much raw material as they can. They have voracious appetites. They connect with other people. They read books. They watch films and take classes and go to new places and try new things. The more we increase our inputs, the more we increase possibilities. The more we cut ourselves off, insulated from new people, new ideas, new flavours and experiences, the more we limit our creative potential.

They say that if you wait until you're thirsty before you drink water, you've already started to dehydrate. The same is true of ideas. It's no good waiting until you're dry before you go looking for new input. But when you're dry, and riding the wave of your creative rhythm off the peaks and into the valleys, increasing your inputs is the only way to make sure you've got the momentum to ride that wave from its lowest point back to the peak.

We're not islands. We don't self-generate ideas. "Out of nothing, nothing comes," also applies here. Seed your garden with everything you can, soak it in, and don't try to force the dots together: just let them sit there. If ideation is about collecting and connecting dots, then it's the collecting which we can do intentionally. The connecting is a passive act of incubation, and that takes time.

INCUBATION

Understanding inspiration as work, as intentional effort, flies in the face of popular meaning, which has more to do with fairy dust and implies that ideas just come out the blue, which they do not. At the best of times, when everything is going well and the cogs are oiled, it might feel that way, as if one moment, with our heads vacant, we were looking around, glassy-eyed, for an idea, and the next moment our minds are swimming with ideas that will change the world. In these moments, thank the gods you've been ingesting new ideas and increasing your inputs, because those, combined with the incubation of time, are what got you here. Fairy dust has nothing to do with it.

This is why so many artists have weighed in on the power of setting to our work to find so-called inspiration. It was the poet Charles Baudelaire who said inspiration comes from working. The painter Chuck Close said inspiration was for amateurs, the rest of us get to work. Because when we get to work we set the cogs in motion and our brains, like boats, are easier to steer while in motion. It's setting ourselves to work that combines the two halves of a messy process—the generation of ideas and the execution of them.

Surprisingly, while we're taught that ideas lead to execution, it's more complicated. Closer to true is that it's cyclical, and a couple of things need to be happening simultaneously. First, we need to be putting as much fuel on the fire as possible. That's increasing our inputs. Then we wait, and those divergent thoughts and ideas—the dots—incubate and eventually, unpredictably, connect and become new ideas. That's ideation. But if we understand incubation to mean we sit around watching the wallpaper peel, we'll be waiting a long time. Instead, while we wait, we work. We keep adding new dots. We work with the ideas already in play. If it's painting, we sit down in front of the canvas and start moving the brush. If it's writing, we put our bodies in the chair and do the work. We show up. We put in the time. That's the execution. And while we faithfully execute, the unborn ideas incubate. They come when they're ready.

The most creative people I know are also the hardest working. I don't think that's a coincidence. Our brains work best when the machinery in the front is working hard and letting the machinery in the back do what it does without too many eyes on it. Doing the work leads to new ideas and on those rare occasions when the idea comes out in the shower, it's only because it couldn't wait until you got around to the day's work.

Give your ideas time. Don't rush them. Let them come. Be patient. But don't wait passively because the brain that is going to connect the dots is only as strong as you make it with the day-to-day effort of your work. It's an astonishing thing, this brain of ours, but it's not magic. And on the flip side, the most creative people I know also understand that time spent staring out the window, napping, having a glass of wine, and being with the ones we love instead of working is not time wasted. This eight-hour workday that we've adopted, and one I've mercifully avoided for most of my life, doesn't serve most of us very well, especially those of us in creative work. It's true that I sometimes work 12 hours instead, so distracted by what I'm doing, so in the momentum of my flow that time passes without my notice. It's also true that there are days I sit down to write and after two hours of productive time, my brain won't go any further, and I need to go for a walk or take a nap, and those activities restore me where pushing through would only shut me down further. It's why ultimately only you can know how you work best, and the sooner you get a sense of how you work most productively, and the sooner you give yourself permission to work this way, the better.

BEGIN

While so-called creatives are often talked about as dreamers with their heads in the clouds, I find it hard to reconcile that with my belief that creativity is about actual creation, not merely ideation. Sure, it's important to have time for great ideas to come your way, and there's a lot you can do to make sure that happens. But mistaking ideation for creation isn't unlike mistaking an architect for a contractor. Both are necessary, but neither does the job of the other.

In order to create, you have to actually make something. In *Linchpin*, Seth Godin calls it "shipping," and he places a great deal of importance on it. Scott Belsky, author of *Making Ideas Happen*, talks about it in terms of living a life with a strong bias towards action. And if the attributions are correct, the poet Goethe says simply, "Begin."

Few things will block the creative process like procrastination, and the more "creative" we are, the easier it is to rationalize that procrastination, to find reasons why it's not only justified, but necessary.

We do it because to honour the work means to do it with excellence, and (this is the voice of procrastination speaking,) if I spend more time sharpening my pencils, and polishing my ideas, the work will be much better. I'll start tomorrow. To quote Ze Frank, "My pencils are sharp enough. Even the dull ones will make a mark."

We do it because "we're not inspired today," so we put it off until tomorrow, never twigging to the reality that the longer we put off our work, the longer the muse stays away, watching from the sidelines while we talk ourselves out of the one thing guaranteed to bring her to our side: work.

We do it because the kids are calling or the dishes need washing. The measure of how desperate we are to avoid beginning our work lies in what otherwise onerous tasks we perform eagerly instead of just sitting down at the potter's wheel, the laptop, the canvas, and starting.

When pushed, we throw the blame at genetics. "I'm just a procrastinator," we say, which is, of course, total crap because most of us just substitute one activity for another. We're substitutors, and if we were more honest with ourselves we'd admit that we're just looking for one more thing to stand in the way so we don't have to look ourselves in the mirror and admit that we're scared of starting yet another thing that comes with the promise of failure, and effort, and the great trauma of being transparent.

I've mentioned this once, but it bears repeating. In his book *The War of Art*, Steven Pressfield talks about fear as though it's a compass, faithfully pointing in the direction of the thing we most need to be doing. So too, our procrastination points to the lodestone of our fears, and as Pressfield points out, the very thing on which we ought to be working.

That one thing may be terrifying. You may have more to lose by attempting this than by spending an hour on Facebook, but all the friends and followers in the world aren't going to make your work better, or get it started on your behalf. And where you have the most to lose, you have the most to gain, so get started. Begin despite the fear. Begin despite your unreadiness. Begin despite your lack of inspiration or growing pile of dishes. Start.

The most prolific writers know that this is not an option. They sit down, often at the same time, in the same place, for the same amount of time, every single day, and they write. It is not optional and there is nothing more important they should be doing right at that moment. Giving yourself the *choice* is where it all unravels for most of us.

I carve out blocks of time and put a line through my calendar, and that time becomes non-negotiable. When I'm writing, I get up at the same time, go to the same coffee shop, listen to the same music, and do my work. There's something comfortable to me about the ritual of it, but it's more than that: it's the self-imposed constraint of non-negotiability. So on days I don't feel well, I get up and write, even if it's crap. On days I feel uninspired, I get up and write, and trust that the muse, if she's out there at all, will show up. On days I've got important things nagging at me, I remind myself that they can wait, and my work cannot. If I put it off today, I will put it off tomorrow, and there will always, always, be something that begs for my attention in the peripheries of my life. Facebook can wait. So can my friends and my family. I'm not writing all day, I'll get to them later, and when I do, they can have my full attention. If I were a brain surgeon the world out there wouldn't be able to interrupt my work, the dry cleaning wouldn't suddenly need to be picked up, and online social media channels would continue to churn in my absence, while I, barely missed, did the one thing no one else can do for me: my work.

Conceiving a child is nothing remotely like carrying it to term and giving birth. They are two different, if not connected, things. Conceiving it, if the growth of our race is any indication, is pretty easy for most. Some have even called it fun. There are people that so enjoy that part of it, that they do it often. But the act of getting the seed planted, when everything works as it should, is nothing like the effort required to do the rest. Make love as often as you've got the stamina for, but don't mistake it for the whole process of creating a child. Ideas are fun to play with, but they're the easy part; they incubate on their own and require little from us but the fertile ground and the, uh, inputs. It's getting that idea birthed into the world from which we run, which is a shame, because by the time it's ready to come out and become truly something, the work becomes the most rewarding. Stop now and what little efforts we give those ideas will be born gasping for air and clutching to life.

Of course most of us know this. We don't come up with ideas that excite us to simply shelve them. Not intentionally. But life happens, and those ideas sit for a while, waiting for the perfect time to begin. The time when we've got all the details figured out, or when we just have more time. The longer those ideas sit, the greater the chance they'll never happen. It's not enough that we simply begin.

We need, most of us, to begin now. When the idea comes and you've got the seed of something that excites you, start right now. While you have some momentum, harness it. While there's fresh energy there, ride that wave over some of the fears that'll settle in when you've had time to sit on it a little. Common sense and the so-called realities of life will drown that spark, and it's the ones quenched by those voices that are the ones our own souls, and the world, most need.

Make a checklist. Sketch it out. Put a line on your calendar. Call a collaborator. Do *something*. The longer you wait, the greater the chance your idea will seem less brilliant, and that's a shame because the light of day, after you've waited a while, is not the time to evaluate your idea. Ideas rarely come out whole. They change as they get brought to life. New constraints appear, new directions suggest themselves, and new influences come to bear. The creative process is a place where evolutions and juxtapositions and unexpected mash-ups occur, but *only once we begin*. It's here the ideas show their true potential to us, often so much more than what we expected. Had we not started when we did there's a chance it never would have happened. It's not that getting to work immediately is our only chance of bringing the idea into the world, it's also that it's often our only chance of making the idea better, proving it and seeing its true genius. The initial idea is a big "what if?" But getting to work on it—and not letting it die out—is where we begin to listen to the answers and find new questions. It's there that the real work of creation begins.

EMBRACING THE CONSTRAINTS

Creativity has always happened best within con-straints. In fact, creativity has often been a response to constraints, not much more, really, than problem solving. For the artist, a lack of constraints would be par-alyzing. When I teach my students to not only embrace their constraints, but to pursue them, by choosing only one lens, only one subject or theme, they find it immedi-ately liberating, and their work becomes more creative.

Most of us do not have to create constraints; we all live and create with enough limitations. Not enough money. Not enough time. Not tall enough. Not smart enough. But there's a fine line between a constraint and an excuse, though often the only difference between them is per-spective, and how we act on them. A constraint seen as a help to the creative process gets us closer to accomplish-ing our work. Seen as a barrier, that constraint becomes an excuse. Like so much in life it's a matter of attitude, though it's taken me over 40 years to see it.

The word "attitude" has always stuck in my throat. Flogged with the word all through school because my attitude never met expectations, it's taken me a long time to get comfortable with the idea that our attitudes matter. Psychology has a lot to say about the effect of the way we think about every aspect of our lives, not because there is magic in it, but because our thinking directs us. Positive thinking, as abused as it is by hucksters and charlatans, is a powerful force, and negative thinking is devastating.

Refusing to embrace our constraints and use them as a creative force can very quickly turn us from artists and creatives into victims. Victims don't make art; they make excuses. We don't make art in the absence of fear, doubt, hurt, financial ruin, broken hearts, sickness and violence, but as a reaction to them. It's the way of the human heart and mind to respond to what life has thrown at us and to keep processing even after the tears have run out and there's no light at the end of the tunnel. For millennia our suffering has been the forge in which great art has been made and great lives have been lived. Returning to the metaphor of the Artist's Journey, it is here we find ourselves in the Innermost Cave, facing the darkness and demons, that we are changed and it's here where we either win or lose. In my experience the innermost cave is no place for excuses and self-pity. They feel good at the time but they work against us.

We all have reasons for not creating the art—or the life—we fantasize about. Some of those reasons are grounded in reality. They're not excuses, they're just life. But they are not reasons to stop creating art at all, or for not living an exceptional life. "I can't paint like Picasso" is just an excuse not to paint to the best of your ability. If Helen Keller, blind, deaf, and mute, could lead an extraordinary life, so can you. If artists can paint with their feet, so can you. If paraplegics can climb some of the world's highest mountains, so can you. Your biggest handicap is a constraint, not an excuse.

If all this sounds like so much chest pounding, then perhaps we could all use a little more chest pounding. I don't subscribe to the idea that our limitations and circumstances stop us from living lives that become art and inspire others, because art isn't always in the finishing but in the trying. You can live a great story without ever reaching your goal, because the journey is in the trying. It's the struggle itself, and while you may not make it to the top of Everest, for most of us it's inspiring enough that you tried, and the story—your story—will still play out in unexpected ways. The story that ends exactly as predicted is the story of the one that doesn't try, for whom their constraints are defining limitations that keep them from ever beginning their art, starting their adventure, or writing their story. All of us make our art in the context of a tough and unpredictable world, full of heartbreak and unfairness. There is no such thing as safety; none of us emerges unscathed. We make our art despite, and even aided by, our constraints, never in the absence of them.

PROCESS VS. PRODUCT

Read much about the art of writing and at some point you're bound to wonder if a certain amount of masochism is required to enter the field. One reader on my blog, commenting on the way I'd been so transparent about my own frustrations (in this case concerning my photography), told me he was no longer interested in reading my blog because my angst exhausted him. And here I thought I was making it look easy. Making art is hard.

One writer said writing was easy: it only required sitting in front of a typewriter and opening a vein. Indeed. I think most things in life, the things that really matter, require us to bleed a little. To put ourselves so thoroughly into something can't be easy. But if it's so hard that we find no joy in it, why bother? For the joy of completion? For the praise of others? Those seem like poor incentives, given how often a work—whatever it is—never gets completed, and how seldom our finished work finds truly honest and lasting praise.

True, there's a thrill in finishing the work, and seeing it published, or hanging on a wall, but too much time spent nurturing an addiction to completion risks rushing through the process of creation itself, sabotaging the very work we aim to see done. It is the process itself where we discover new things, and find the first hints about new directions. Very little work becomes, in the end, the thing we imagined it to be at the beginning. Like the artist that makes it, it evolves, reacts, and becomes something more than we once expected. Unless, in rushing to the end, we miss those chances to not only take the work in new directions, but to enjoy the process, and savour the challenge. It might not be enjoyment in the same way we enjoy a good glass of wine, but it can be a deep-down sense of being alive, of being stretched, of knowing you can do this without having the foggiest idea exactly how.

The same sabotage of process happens when we create merely for the praise of others. It's true: even as adults, most of us long in some way to have our art put on the fridge and praised. There's a thrill to knowing something we've done has struck a chord with others, and means something to someone outside our own heads. Who doesn't long to be relevant, to be noticed? But if that's where you find the joy, and not in the creative process itself, then it's as likely as not that you'll sabotage your own work.

Creativity carries with it, necessarily, that sense of "this might not work." And freed from that, and from the frisson that comes with risk, putting yourself out there, and into this thing you're making, whatever it is, the work loses its spark. There can be no guarantee that anything we create will be praised, or even understood, so to labour through a process you do not love, and in which you find no joy, only to create something that may never bring you the adulation you want, or need, seems a waste of the few, uncertain days we have on this earth. Better to find something you love doing, and do it for the love of it, than to work so hard for an insatiable ego making something that might never feed it. Even when we do make something that strikes a chord, praise fades quickly and has diminishing returns.

Creation is work, at times hard work, and the product of our creative process often yields a low return on the investment. We sure as hell better love the process, and find some joy in the struggle itself because we'll spend much more of our lives actively creating than we ever will looking at the final piece, or hearing how good it is from the lips of others. Pragmatically I'm arguing for more than just a feel-good love of the labour, though that's reason enough to create. A preoccupation with the end product of our efforts takes us from the present moment in which we need to give ourselves over to the process, and robs us of the very thing we long for: finished work that's bigger or better than we dared hope for. It is this way whether that work is a story, a painting, or raising a child. Art is created in the present, where nothing is guaranteed to us but the process of making it. If we stay in that moment and enjoy the full experience of it—if not because of the challenge then despite it—our work will be better for it.

MORE BAD IDEAS

There might be a reason why some writers prefer to exercise their craft while following Hemingway's advice to "Write drunk; edit sober." Whether the approach is healthy or not, I can't say, but the ability of a stiff drink to lower our inhibitions has been celebrated by many in their search for good ideas. Now, let me state categorically, that very few of my best ideas have come from a bottle. I wrote one of my books while recovering from two broken feet, and I can tell you the morphine only made things more challenging for my editor. However, alcohol does more than just keep the liver distracted. It has a way of quieting the inner censor, which I think was the point Hemingway was making.

Almost all of us have an inner voice whose self-appointed role in our lives is protecting us from ourselves and our bad ideas. The moment it catches wind that we're working on something new it begins dropping the filters into place, trying desperately to stop our half-baked ideas from getting out into the world and embarrassing us.

Without this voice we might be saved from some small social faux pas and a few awkward moments, but also from some truly great ideas. But we'll never fully know because those ideas never had a chance to become what they might have been. That inner censor may be very self-protective, but it's rubbish at understanding how ideas work. Free of this understanding, it unknowingly kills a great many beautiful notions before they ever have a chance.

Consider this truly trite but relevant metaphor: you love butterflies and want one very badly. Without understanding how metamorphosis works, but knowing very well that you do not like caterpillars, you step on each one you find. It could be a long time indeed before you get what you're after. Dead caterpillars lead to very few butterflies. I warned you it was trite. But I'd rather my metaphor work for you than be particularly poetic or profound. Bad ideas are like caterpillars.

Good ideas, on balance, do not simply appear from the ether. Ignoring for a moment the role of work and so-called inspiration, they come from the relentless generation of many ideas, and of those, most are mediocre, if not outright lousy. I'm not suggesting all ideas are good ideas, but they are useful. Because it is the mind that is encouraged to take the bad ideas, suspend judgment for a time, and follow the trail to see where they lead in order to find more good ideas. An idea may in fact be completely unworkable, but combine it with another impractical idea and you might have something astonishing.

It's important to understand how metamorphosis works. Creativity has been described as the simple ability to make unlikely connections. These are the dots that Steve Jobs talked about, and here it is quantity that matters, not quality. The quality comes, not from the dots themselves, but from your ability to see, and follow, the combinations of connections. It comes from a relentless ability to collect these dots and keep them around, without judging them good or bad. One combination may be less workable than another, but if working through the less workable solutions is what got you to a connection between others, changing them from two or three so-called bad ideas into one beautiful idea, then the bad ideas aren't bad at all, just necessary raw materials.

It would be a mistake, however, to assume the inner censor is purely negative. It's often the voice saying, "That's a dumb idea, stop now." But get on a roll and it'll be the one saying, "That's a good idea, maybe you should quit while you're ahead." Either way, it's just a voice and there's no reason in the world not to tell it to shut the hell up. To return to Hemingway, you're drunk (metaphorically), you're writing, you're on a roll. Don't you dare stop now; you can stop later when you sober up and begin to edit. But right now, order another (metaphorical) drink and keep going. Connect those dots like a man on fire. Now is not the time to be tentative, to worry about your reputation, or to fear failure.

In my younger days I did improv comedy, from which, at the expense of paying audiences to whom I now feel somewhat apologetic, I learned more about the creative process than I did about acting. One of the guiding principles of improv is "Say yes." Go with it. Whatever you do, don't say no. No stops things dead in their tracks. No blocks possibility and makes for very short, very unfunny improv. Ideas move *forward* very well. It is their natural state to move quickly, to change when exposed to new ideas, and become something else. Without the forward momentum of Yes, they die.

I carry with me a Moleskine notebook. It goes everywhere with me, along with my camera, and both the camera and the notebook are full to busting with some very bad ideas. My process with the camera is to create visual notes, or sketch images. They're the ones people will sift through after my death, shaking their heads at the vast amounts of mediocrity I was able to create in only one lifetime. But they aren't really mediocre, just misunderstood. They're raw materials. They're the record of me playing with lines, light, balance, tension, moments, and the way my lenses change all of those. In my notebooks the so-called bad ideas are the record of my playing with thoughts and words. That play almost always begins with old, repeated, or obvious ideas. But it often leads to the favourite question of every curious person: What if I...?

You can't judge the raw materials the way you evaluate a finished product. As a novel, it might stink, but as a first draft it's full of possibility and questions. As a painting it might not work, but as a series of sketches, there's a new idea that merits exploration. As a meal it might be truly offensive, but if there's a new combination of flavours and textures that will work brilliantly in something else, then it's part of your creative process. We ought not be so hard on things unfinished, and that includes ourselves.

It's because the raw materials differ so much from the final product, and are so necessarily undeveloped, half-baked, and yes, even stupid, that we need to silence the censors who would stop their creation entirely. If it takes a glass of whisky, so be it.

THE STARVING ARTIST

Embracing our constraints (and refusing to be a victim of them) does not mean passive acceptance. Debt—and other financial issues—is one of those constraints. A great deal of art has been made by the prototypical starving artist, but that doesn't mean you have to turn yourself into one. You can live an extraordinary life under the weight of debt, but getting out from that weight is an even better story.

On February 14, 2006, I walked into a trustee's office and with one signature became bankrupt. Years of debt had spiralled out of control, to the point where even with a good living at the top of my career as a comedian I couldn't get any further than the minimum payments, and the interest was piling up. I was given mountains of paperwork to fill out and on the line that said "Reason for Bankruptcy," I put one word: optimism.

Going bankrupt wasn't my first choice. I'd gotten on top of my spending, but even without adding to the debt, the interest was accumulating. I'd gone in for credit counselling and, after laying my embarrassing financial situation out, was told I had two options: a credit proposal that would allow me to renegotiate my debt, or bankruptcy. I chose the credit proposal. I was then sent to a trustee to deal with the paperwork and she also told me that I had two options, but this time the options were different. Because I was self-employed (as a comedian, no less), I had no chance of getting my credit proposal approved, so my new options were these: go bankrupt this month, or go bankrupt *next* month. Happy Valentine's Day.

Years later I can see two things with much greater clarity. The first is how much I allowed the clamour of a culture of conspicuous consumption to dictate my spending habits, which led me into uncontrolled credit spending, as I knew my prospects were improving imminently. They weren't—at least not faster than my spending. The second is how much freedom I now have, and will always have, because I will never go into debt again. I know I was told as a kid that borrowing money made you beholden to the lender but clearly I didn't absorb the lesson in ways that were anything but theoretical. I'd somehow accumulated an astonishing amount of credit debt with nothing to show for it, and that debt had begun to severely limit what I could do. I had traded against my future for the shiny toys of the present, and when the future showed up I was still paying for the toys, now broken or forsaken in favour of something newer, also paid for by my future self.

Talking about money is not easy. But it has to be said, though I'll keep it short. If it helps, think of this as a bit of a distracted sidebar. In the broadest possible sense, the appetites of our culture have outgrown what we're able to swallow, yet alone afford. Though time is not money, it's like it in the sense that most of us have only so much of it. We can't afford everything. But the things we hunger for—the bucket list items and the bigger dreams—always seem just a little less immediately accessible than the larger television or the new sofa. When people say they wish they could do the things I do with my time (usually travel), they usually mean they wish they could do what I do while still maintaining the lifestyle they've chosen, a lifestyle I couldn't afford if I wanted to do what I do. I don't have unlimited money any more than anyone else forced to choose between one dream and another: we want it all. But as the prophet Jagger said, "You can't always get what you want, but if you try sometimes, you might find you get what you need." A wise man, that guy.

I read somewhere that there are two ways to get what you want. The first is to acquire more and more. The second is to desire less and less. Why this matters in the context of living our lives creatively and intentionally is that, in light of the fact that we can't have it all, every dream we have requires a choice. That choice is removed from us in the present when we're paying for the decisions we made in the past. Without exaggeration, the greatest freedom I've ever experienced is the sudden loss of the debt that was draining me. I only wish I'd had that freedom much sooner.

The problem is not debt. Debt is the symptom. The problem is our appetite and an overly optimistic hope for tomorrow's finances, against which we're borrowing. Of course the money we've got doesn't feed today's appetites, so there's no way—short of a windfall, and that's the voice of optimism, not reality—it will be enough tomorrow, never mind enough to also pay for the debt we're collecting. To say no to debt and "later" to our appetites is an act of anarchy that leads to greater freedom. But it's not easy. We measure ourselves—often *define* ourselves—by our acquisitions. We so identify with brand messaging that we don't feel we're being true to ourselves unless we drive the right car, wear the right clothes, or use the latest, and right, computer.

The problem: it's not sustainable. It's not sustainable on a global level, and it's not sustainable personally. If you want to live with greater freedom you need to control your appetite. And if you can't do that, you need to control the spending that feeds your appetite. Buy the new iPhone, but do it with the money you have today because the debt you're adding to will last much longer than the iPhone will. And then you'll need another iPhone you still can't afford.

How many generations of iPhones can you afford to pay for in the future? Wouldn't you rather spend that money on a trip to Nepal or Paris? Wouldn't you rather have money in savings to take a year off and write the novel you long to write? Wouldn't most of us be happier with a smaller television or an older car (or neither), and a chance to swim with the dolphins or get to Everest Base Camp instead? I'm going to go with "yes," because if the answer's "no," then you aren't reading this book right now. You've long given up and are watching reruns of *Lost* on TV right now. But none of those things are going to happen on their own.

Where were the courses on how not to be a moron with my money when I was in school? Why did I never absorb the lessons that were there? If I'm honest, it's not because I wasn't taught; I just didn't learn. What I learned was it would be wise to save my money. It would be wise to remain out of debt. But I wasn't interested in wisdom. I was interested in experiences, and I wonder what would have happened if I'd been told I could be driving a Ferrari when I was 18 if I wanted to. No kid wants a savings account. Every boy wants a Ferrari, even if that particular Ferrari isn't a red Italian sports car.

It comes back to the question, "What do I want?" In my forties I have clearer answers to that question. I don't want a Ferrari. But I want freedom. Freedom to travel. To create. To live my so-called bucket list. To do good in this world, and to help the people closest to me to do the same. I can't do that with debt.

Debt cripples me where I should otherwise be free, and I will never again be bound by it. Where money is concerned, that is my biggest desire and I work hard to remain in that place. It means paying cash for things, and never carrying a balance on my credit card. It means making choices, and though it can be argued that my income is now consistent enough that it's an easy sermon for me to preach, it should be pretty obvious that this is all relative. People of every income bracket seem to find it difficult, regardless of the size of their paycheque, to live within their means. In fact, it seems the larger the paycheque, the greater the gulf between what's getting earned and what's getting spent. Our appetites grow exponentially if we allow them to.

Whatever else it is, this is not a book about finances. But it is a book about the freedom to live your creative life to the fullest, and you'd be insane to believe that living in obedience to debt and under the tyranny of bill collectors is your best possible creative space. I also think this particular discussion dovetails well with the discussion on fear because so many of us spend the way we do to fill empty spaces in our lives, or to placate the fears: fear of not fitting in; fear of missing out; fear of the way others see us. If we're willing to face those fears for what they are and stop feeding the hunger those fears create, it becomes a little easier to get our financial house in order and stop leveraging the future to pay for our past and present lust.

If you're looking for more, all I can suggest is a path similar to the one I took. What you do with your debt is up to you, and I'm not necessarily suggesting you go bankrupt. I'm suggesting you learn as much as you can about money. Take a deep breath, swallow your pride, and call a debt counsellor. Go to the library and check out titles on personal financial management. Read books like *The Richest Man in Babylon*, which is aging and a little contrived but contains solid wisdom. Find someone you respect who has their financial house in order and ask them how they did it. Look for wisdom. Renegotiate your debt, get rid of the credit cards that charge you criminal rates of interest, and put the other credit card in a block of ice in the freezer. Learn to live within your means: the freedom it brings you will be worth the overhaul it requires to get there.

Whatever you choose to do, don't let your optimism get the best of you. This is one area where being conservative more than you are optimistic will pay solid dividends. Things might be getting better, your prospects might be improving, and you might truly be about to "make it." Just because there's suddenly more food on the table doesn't mean you should eat more. Use the growth to be more aggressive about eliminating your debt, keep the taxman happy, and save, but not as an excuse to go out and buy something. Celebrate when the debt is gone, not now.

THE ART OF EXCLUSION

If life is short, then it follows that there is more to do in our brief, beautiful days than we could ever accomplish.

It is said that photography is the art of exclusion. What the photographer leaves out of the frame is as important as what he leaves in. Within the frame of the photograph every element pulls the eye, and though not every element demands our attention in the same way, there is only so much impact a frame can contain; the more the included elements compete for that impact, the less impact any one part of the frame can have. That is to say, the photograph is stronger for the photographer's ability to say no.

The photographer who wants to move hearts or change minds knows that saying yes to all the possible elements and letting them all into the frame is not an act of generosity: it's a refusal to allow the most important elements to play with the strength with which they're capable.

No one can do it all, but the pressure to try is paralyzing. And so we say yes to a million efforts that pull us in a million directions, and say no to the most important things in our lives by our refusal to give them the time they need.

But we keep saying yes because we want our lives to have impact. We want to make a difference. We want to love others. But what impact can we have if, by diluting ourselves over a thousand trivialities and the tasks of others, we leave our work undone, or done with less than our full attention and energy? Saying no seems so selfish, but so be it. I don't think there are many lives so full that we can't extend ourselves generously to others, so perhaps there's a middle ground. If you have trouble saying no to others, I want you to look around, make sure no one's listening, and repeat after me: "I would love to help you. I'm in the middle of a project right now that requires all of my attention. I can give you an hour tomorrow." Now say it again (this time say it for real, because I know most of you just cheated). Does it have to be tomorrow? No. But give it some time because if it's really, truly important they'll be glad for the help, even tomorrow, and if it's really urgent, they'll find someone else before then. Do your work first.

Imagine having unlimited funds. You'd give money to almost anyone that asked, wouldn't you? But now imagine you've got money in your pocket but have no idea how much is there. How carefully then would you give it away? What would you choose to spend it on, and to whom or what would you say no? You can say no with a smile. You can apologize. You can be kind about it. But every time soneone places a demand on your time that does not serve you, your work, and the people and causes that mean the most in this world to you, they are asking an audacious thing when they ask, unblinking, to take a piece of your most precious commodity.

Guard your time fiercely. Be generous with it, but be intentional about it. Guard it the same way you guard your money. It's the one resource with which we have increasingly less to do our life's work, and to be with those we love. Say yes to those things first.

WAITING FOR THE KNOCK

A friend of mine is a comedian. He's been making people around the world laugh for over thirty years. He's very good and very funny. And he goes home after every gig, these days after long weeks of entertaining on large cruise ships, and when his wife asks him how it went he tells her the same thing—"I still didn't get the knock." "The knock?" I once asked. "Yeah, you know, the knock. When someone comes to your dressing room and knocks and tells you they've discovered you have no talent and want you to leave." Ah yes, the knock.

How many of us feel like we're faking it? In those moments when I'm totally transparent and feeling brave, I'll tell you it's one of the two fears with which I wrestle daily: the first that one day I'll wake to find my muse has abandoned me and that I've shot my last good photograph, written my last decent sentence; and the second is that one day everyone will all wake up to the collective revelation that I'm just faking it. The fear, at least the second one, is like most fear: it's bullshit. But there's also a little truth in it.

Because I *am* faking it. We all are. We're making it up as we go. That's what creative people in any pursuit do. It's not a part of what we do, it's the very *nature* of what we do. We try new things, go where we've never gone, and do things for which there are neither rules nor established ways we *should* do what we do. In the process we make a lot of mistakes, fall on our faces, and—in the case of photographers—we make a lot of really bad photographs, or sketch images, in pursuit of the good ones. The public, whoever that is, only sees the good stuff. We see it all: the crap, the dross, the chaff, and it's often the flotsam and jetsam of the creative process that we get hung up on, forgetting that every artist creates the same waste as they chase their own muse. The more creative we are (or endeavour to be), the more of it—the crap, the evidence of our faking it—we produce. It's part of the process. The alternative is following patterns, colouring within the lines, covering territory we've covered a million times before, and taking no risks.

It's easy to look at someone who fits our own understanding of what it means to have succeeded, and to assume they no longer battle these demons, but your view of any artist, or any human in any field of endeavour, is as muddled as his or her own view of themselves. You see a photographer who's made it. Published books. Worked for great clients. Created something for which they've received accolades or, God help them, awards. And you assume he no longer fears the knock, the one where they come to tell him he's finally been fingered for faking it. The thing is, he fears it *more*. Because most often the artist (and I've yet to meet one so well adjusted that I can say there are exceptions to this) just sees his success as a string of flukes, hard work, and probably a little mistaken identity. It isn't the faking it–artist I worry about; it's the one who thinks he isn't.

Why I think this matters is because when we begin to see this as normal, as part of the inner life of the artist, we can stop beating ourselves up for it. We can take the proper place of the artist—a posture of humility before the muse—knowing we are dependent not on our gifts or talents or painfully waiting for inspiration from above, but on hard work and circumstance and the mystery of the creative process.

There is great freedom in knowing we might never *make* it, even when in the eyes of so many we already have. Or we might already be there and never see it. I suspect it's a little of both, depending on what day it is, because "to make it" is so subjective. For me the goal is not to make it but to *be making it*. To live a life of daily creation, where the "it" changes often. To every day find new ways to "fake it" and see if that leads to something beautiful, knowing that if the knock comes, the imagined accusers on the other side of the door can tell us nothing we've not told the world already and tried, every day, to own. We're faking it. Of course we are. You should expect nothing else but that we do so honestly, intentionally, and with our whole hearts.

I think there's also another sense in which we feel a fraud, and that's the issue of qualification. In most fields of endeavour there is a standard of experience or education that you either meet, or not. And no matter what anyone tells you there is no such standard of qualification to be a human being or an artist. It is enough that you are human, that you experience this life in ways common to us all and unique to yourself, and that you do your work.

Qualification matters in one sense only: the acceptance of peers. And I'd wager in the grand scheme of things, our art—whatever that means to you—is better created outside those circles than within them. Perhaps you feel talent is the qualification you lack. And you know what, maybe you're right. The fact is there are some very talented human beings on this planet—people who, through some astonishing genetic fluke, can do what they do in ways most of us never imagined. Lucky them.

Most of us will get by just fine without half their talent, and many of us will get further, by doing our work and leaving the question of talent to the philosophers. You are more talented than some, and if you're like me, you're less talented (whatever that means) than many. Fine. Now that that's out of the way, do your work. Talent doesn't qualify you to do your art. Doing your art is what qualifies you to do your art.

Of course there's a sense in which we're not faking it at all, and I know those words make some feel uncomfortable. I'm talking about the honest admission that we're making this up as we go, even if that improvisation comes on twenty years of experience and a certain expertise. Whatever you call it, improvisation makes us all feel a little nervous, and feeling like a fraud is the natural result of not only improvising, but also getting away with it. When the world at large and the prevailing culture honours road maps and implied rules, those who succeed by following their intuition and a voice that won't stop asking "What if?" are bound to feel a little like they've cheated. It'll pass. Or it won't. But don't let it sideline you. The real fraud isn't asking the question or being haunted by the doubts. Waiting for the knock keeps us honest.

KNOW YOUR RHYTHM

Every person I know—whether they identify as creative or not—goes through ups and downs, though I think the self-identifying creative or artist can feel it more acutely, as though our creative life rides on top of the water and rises and falls with the waves. We experience brilliant highs and depressing lows. When the wind kicks up and the ocean is wild, the highs are higher, and we feel glorious, unstoppable, and they crash harder, the glory gone. Stopped.

What helps is not looking too closely at the wave, but at the ocean itself. Pull back, look at the water from a hill ten miles distant and the water looks smooth as glass—as your creative life does, or will, from a distance. The dips and peaks evened out. This helps not because it makes one bit of difference when you're at the bottom of a wave cycle and you feel like you've made your last good, beautiful, photograph or written your last honest word. It helps because it allows us to understand the cycle, to use it, to ride out the waves, even building momentum.

Our creative life, the very nature of how most of us work internally, is rhythmic. Brilliant creativity is unsustainable day to day. A wave that has a high, but is not flanked by lows, is not a wave: it's placid water. No lows, but no highs, either. We have a word for it in the creative world: mediocrity. In his book *The Accidental Creative,* Todd Henry says, "Mediocrity is a high price to pay for a lifetime of safety." You can't have this creative life, ask for the highs, and never get the lows. That doesn't make the lows easier, but it's nice to feel normal, isn't it?

Creativity happens in the space between taking in and incubating as many influences as the world allows us, and the sudden rush of a newborn idea that comes into the world in a mix of hard work and joy, sweat, and tears. The birth of that idea, and the execution of it, are often on the crest of the wave. They are the high points for which we live. If the high point of that wave is adoration and praise, then you're missing out. Singer/songwriter Josh Ritter sings, "I'm singing for the love of it, have mercy on the man who sings to be adored." Russian actor (and originator of Method acting) Konstantin Stanislavski, said, "Love the art in yourself, not yourself in the art." But that's a digression, not really my point.

My long-winded point is this: it's in the lows of the wave where we feed inspiration. If we are conscious of the shape of the wave and the way our process works, we know that wave will crest again. What we do at the bottom of the wave determines how much momentum we have at the top. We can spend that time being depressed and feeling sorry for ourselves, or we can feed the muse, take our Sabbath rest. We can go to the museum, the gallery, the coffee shop, the library, the theatre, or wherever it is you find your own paint stirred. Forget how you've suddenly lost your brilliance. Go find the brilliance of others and let it feed your soul. Go be with your family, read a book, and then, most importantly, do the work. Don't set your camera down simply because inspiration hasn't yet come.

Riding these waves gets more predictable the longer you do it; you see the rhythm in it, you begin to know your process. I will often mumble this to myself in the lows, when I am doing the work and my muse (wretched, unreliable, prodigal muse, where the hell is she?!) is nowhere in sight. "Trust your process, David. It'll come." And I keep working, mumbling other things, less savory and less family-rated things, but I keep at it, and the movement of the wave carries me forward, pulls me upward, as it always does, and I begin to get excited about what

I might find at the top, and I get more grateful for the muse (wonderful, reliable, always-present muse!).

Be conscious of the highs and lows and give yourself the grace to learn to ride those waves. It's easy to write about it, sitting here myself when the wave feels high and strong. But when we are in the lowest parts, thrashing about and choking on the surf, it doesn't feel like an inevitable part of our rhythm. It sure as hell doesn't feel like part of a process that will again pull us back to the crest of the wave. It feels lonely and dark and uninspired, and every single person I know goes through it; those creating work that is the most personal, that feels the most as if everything is on the line, feel it the most. There's no way around it but through it. But if you can hold on to a little perspective, recall the way this cycle has resolved in the past, it can give you hope. And when the lows are so low you feel your soul is about to drown, it helps a little to know that you're in the innermost cave again, and this is where you do the hard battle. Will it help if I tell you now that your art will be better for it, and your story stronger? I doubt it. But it will be. And the surge will pull you out the way it always does. Chances are we're both in a valley, separated by only one wave. We'll make it. Let's try not to swallow too much water.

THE MYTH OF ORIGINALITY

*"Millions of men have lived to fight, build palaces
and boundaries, shape destinies and societies; but
the compelling force of all times has been the force of
originality and creation profoundly affecting the roots
of human spirit."*

~ Ansel Adams

The word "originality" has too many meanings in play for me to really trust it. The way Ansel Adams says it makes me want to stand up and cheer, but I'm barely out my seat when, out of the side of his mouth, M.C. Escher whispers, "Originality is merely an illusion," and I sit back down, glad I didn't embarrass myself.

Then Herman Melville takes umbrage, turns to Escher and says, "It is better to fail in originality than to succeed in imitation," before Ezra Pound joins the fray and shuts it all down, dismissively stating that "Utter originality is, of course, out of the question."

I leave and C.S. Lewis passes me a note on the way out. Scribbled, it says, "Even in literature and art, no man who bothers about originality will ever be original: whereas if you simply try to tell the truth (without caring twopence how often it has been told before) you will, nine times out of ten, become original without ever having noticed it."

The pursuit of originality has never interested me much, in part because until we define our terms, it seems like a moving target at which I haven't yet found a good reason to aim. By *it*, do we mean that it's unlike anything else, a completely new thing? For some people this means more than it does to others. For the artist, it's often more important they create something apparently original than that they create something honest or beautiful. Few people, I think, are deeply moved by novelty.

But free from the need to create something novel, there's a sense in which we are free to create something faithful to its origins—which is to say, faithful to us. If "original" can be taken to mean "honest" or "authentic," then I think that's a pursuit worth discussing. "Is it Art?" isn't remotely as interesting to me as "Is it *your* art?" Is it you? Is it what you want? Is it worth so much to you that you're willing to spend your time, effort, and probably a few tears on it? Authenticity trumps novelty every time. But it's so, so much easier said than done.

Authenticity is about one thing: honesty. Is it you? Tough question, I know. Who we are is always changing. Martin Luther once said that this life is not about being but becoming. It's splitting hairs, I know, but it's helpful to remember that we are growing into ourselves as humans, and as artists. I used to snicker when artists said their work was an exploration of this or that. But now I get it. All our work is an exploration. And exploration changes us. It opens our eyes, changes our minds, and makes us think new thoughts. I am not the person I was. My vision changes. And then, necessarily, so does my voice.

Imagine a writer. The stories he writes in his childhood will be about different struggles than in his teens, young adulthood, and the late years of his life. So too will the words change. He may, in his thirties, switch for a while to poetry. A different voice, to be sure, but not necessarily less authentic. In fact, he could discover in poetry his most authentic voice because it allows him to say things in ways he never could in his novels. My favourite writers, like the characters in their stories, change with the arc of their lives, and so too do their voices. But the best of them, the ones that resonate, remain authentic. Genuine. To be authentic is not to be homogenous.

Chasing authenticity is like chasing originality. Spend too much time doing it and you'll lose sight of the thing you were aiming for. It helps not to be too self-conscious. It's the kind of thing that's seen peripherally; it's not seen so easily when you look at it head on. Don't overthink it. Explore. Play. Follow your gut. You'll know when it's you and when it's not. But don't mistake the goal. The goal is to make work that is consistent with who you are and are becoming, not who you once were. Repetition is not the same thing as consistency. It's as easy to be inauthentic by not keeping up with who you are, as it to be so by copying others. Copying others is helpful, even necessary, as we learn, but not so helpful when it comes to making our art. You just have to know the difference. Learn to write like Hemingway. But when you write your novel, adapt what you learn to who you are, not the other way around. Learn to play guitar like Bruce Cockburn, but then write and play your own songs, which will be better for what you've learned.

Don't let the pressure to be original paralyze you or steal your joy. Our highest art is making a life that aligns with who we are, real and whole, if not messy and a little rough around the edges. Originality is a chimera. It's hard enough being you, and being vulnerable enough to be so without hiding behind masks and walls. Put that into your work and your relationships, and the art of your life, and it will be original in the truest sense: it will be you. If that's not good enough for the critics, to hell with them. You can't please everyone.

RUTS & GROOVES

There is a state of creative process, a place in the rhythm of our lives that psychologist Mihaly Csikszentmihalyi calls *flow*. It's a way of working, a state of being when we're fully immersed in what we're doing, fully present, and the usual barriers to our work just seem to step aside. When flow happens it feels like time stops, only catching up to us again when flow stops and it comes hurtling back at us, and we find it's hours later than we thought it was.

Flow is an enviable state, one in which most of us wish we spent more time, but if flow happens only at the crest of the wave, then as much as it's possible we should stack the deck and make sure that wave comes around again by increasing the inputs, exposing ourselves to divergent influences, having more conversations, allowing for incubation time, and most importantly, doing the work; it's impossible to remain there or force it to come around again according to our own timing. Flow doesn't happen when we chase it down. It seems to prefer to be wooed. Flow is not just the coming of the muse; it's when she arrives with such force that she blows the doors off.

Flow is a groove that channels our energy and allows us to put our foot a little harder on the gas without spending quite so much energy worrying about the steering, which in a state of flow feels intuitive, subconscious. But flow comes and goes and it's good it does because the only thing it takes for a groove to become a rut is repeatedly taking the same path, which is tempting when we long for a return to flow more than we long to do the hard work. Ruts require no steering, and the deeper they become the harder it is to climb out. Ruts happen when we look to what's been done before instead of what's untried. They happen when we rest on past victories instead of going out to meet the enemy on whatever battlefield we find him today as we begin our work.

In ruts there is no risk to our creative pursuits, except the risk of repetition, to which I've never known the muse to call me. Life is about change. Art is about change. And if our work changes us, it takes us to new places. Ruts are a sign that we're in the same safe place. No, it wasn't always safe. When we first got there, there was risk, adventure, and that energy translated to some of the best work we've ever done. We made bold moves. We felt the flow. And we made camp, not noticing that the flow, as it does, moved on. We went to bed in a groove, and unwilling to move on, woke up in a rut.

To tie this loosely to the theme of the book, ruts become a controlling force to which we either submit and allow our creative efforts to suffer, or in whose face we rebel, turning the wheel hard in another direction, refusing its rule and jumping the rut. I wish I could tell you how to capture flow and keep it in a bottle, but that's against its very nature. The only thing is to keep moving, don't look back, and do your work. And don't spin your wheels, it'll only dig you in deeper.

WINNING AT YOGA

My immediate world, the world of photography, has a strange obsession with competition. Wherever I look there's a new competition promising big shiny prizes to the best young photographer, travel photographer, wedding photographer, portrait photographer, and on and on. It's not a phenomenon unique to photographers, I know. I'm not sure what the word "best" means in the context of art, but there's no doubt that artists of all stripes have been competing in one way or another since the first two cave men compared the size of their pigment-stained handprints on the wall of the rock hole in which they lived: mine's bigger than yours. Indeed. We're a competitive race. No doubt it comes from the necessarily competitive nature of survival; it's probably thanks to that competitive streak that we've come so far. Go, team, go.

But the creative life is something different and I'm not sure it benefits from that more primal need to be the best. I'm pretty sure anchoring art—which calls us to something more as a species—in competition only holds back the art. It binds us in the very areas our art should be liberating us.

The most enduring art has so endured, in part, because it has the indelible fingerprints of the artist on it, or within it. It is produced from somewhere within a unique person, expressed through some level of competence in their chosen craft, and pushed into the world because the artist could do no other. It may lie unrecognized for generations, may never find public acclaim, may never earn a dollar, but it's uncompromisingly their own. Competition encourages us not to look in but look out, to create not first to please ourselves or express some ineffable thing, but to please another. What magic, I wonder, do we attribute to these judges that they can pin a ribbon, a score out of ten, on this work and not that? What criteria can they possibly be using? Imagine Monet and his impressionist colleagues enduring the mockery of the artistic elite, the Paris Salon (which they did). Imagine our loss had they listened to the harsh condemnation of this new way of seeing and expressing beauty and packed it in, gave up.

Whatever benefit competition has in fuelling a hunger in us to move forward and do our best, it is outweighed by its power to be self-sabotaging. The artist longing to create, the mother longing to raise a child, or the entrepreneur beginning a new enterprise all do well to cast a suspicious eye at competition because making great art is hard enough without comparing ourselves to others. Living an intentional life and making art of our lives has nothing whatsoever to do with what others are doing. That's a distorted mirror in which we'll never look anything but misproportioned.

You don't win at art or life any more than you can win at yoga. They are incompatible paradigms. Comparing ourselves with others plants seeds of envy, jealousy, discouragement, doubt, and fear. It gives way in one direction to self-loathing and in the other to arrogance. In neither of those directions is our best work created.

If competition is natural, part of a long-residual DNA, it does not follow that it is what is best for us. I'm not sure that giving in to every one of our most fundamental urges is healthy. Revenge is one of those urges. It's why forgiveness is so hard. One is instinct; the other is a grace. To be human is to choose, and choosing to compare ourselves with others and base both our beliefs about ourselves, and our actions, on those comparisons is a waste of creative energy—energy that could be used to create something.

Physically, we tend to move in the direction we look. Comparisons are made looking to the side or backwards, but not forward in the direction we long to move. It's a good way to trip over something, or worse, to find ourselves in a rut we never chose on our way to a destination we never set our hearts on, while the thing we most long to do drifts off, divergent, into the distance.

Singer/songwriter Bruce Cockburn put it well when he sang, "Can it be so hard / to love yourself without thinking / someone else holds a lower card?" Let it go. Right now there are millions of people creating astonishing lives and accomplishing things neither you nor I can imagine. I will never be Einstein, or Mother Teresa, or Richard Branson. But wishing I were is the fastest way to make sure I will never be the one thing at which I have a real shot—being fully and completely me, someone who no one else on this planet can be.

I don't yet know the man I am capable of being or the things I am capable of achieving. I do know that the answer won't be found out there on the path of another, no matter how much I covet their talent, their health, their money. They have their own battles to wage, their own constraints to keep them moving forward.

Make your art, and allow yourself to be inspired by theirs. Life is too short to worry about how you stack up: it's not a race. The reward is in the work itself, and the discovery in that work of the person you're becoming.

ART AS GIFT

One of my favourite acts of rebellion in the great narratives of history is the Hebrew flight from Egypt thousands of years ago, under the leadership of Moses. The biblical version goes like this: tired of the tyranny of Pharaoh and the effects of slavery on the people he comes to lead, Moses says let my people go, Pharaoh says no, and then God wipes out every firstborn as the final act of an escalating series of plagues. Gruesome stuff.

Fast forward to the desert. The escaped Hebrews—up to a million strong—are now wandering aimlessly, and hungry. So God provides a food they call manna, a word meaning, "What the heck is this stuff?" Seriously, that's what it means. Though I doubt the word "heck" is a literal translation.

Manna was a flaky food, and while it's called bread, it seems that might only have been the closest thing to compare it to. God provides it daily. Enough for everyone.

But there's a catch. With the exception of the Sabbath they're told they can't store it. They have to trust that it will be there the next day. And the next. And the next. Eat it while you have it, because it turns putrid overnight.

I think there are some intangible things in life that come to us from beyond ourselves, that are meant to be exercised and used as we're given them, with no stockpiling allowed. I think faith is like this, whether its object is God or other people. Love, too. Hope, certainly. And creativity.

Creativity is like manna: it doesn't store well. It comes from somewhere outside ourselves, a gift where every ounce of it is meant to be used, without thought for tomorrow. Don't pace yourself, don't stockpile, and don't hoard it. Use it while you have it. Act on it while the idea makes sense. Remember that creative inhalation (inspiration) can only happen with the same frequency as exhalation (execution). Creativity grows with the expenditure and shrinks with the hoarding. Try to hang on to it without doing the work and it'll turn to dust. Good ideas build on each other and lead to new ideas, but keep them in a box and even those ideas fade away. Use it (now) or lose it.

The source of our creativity is like water. From a spring or deep well, the water keeps flowing. We take what we need; it flows on. It'll be there when we need it. But put the water into a cistern, fearful the well will dry up, and that water becomes stagnant. It's got to keep moving. The gift comes to us, we make something of it, and in turn it makes something of us, and what we make touches others and keeps moving, accumulating the fingerprints of those that touch it. At some point my analogies fail me, but if you want to be more creative, don't hold too tight. If you want to live an extraordinary life (whatever that means for you), let the gift keep moving. A closed heart is the same thing as a closed mind.

NOW

It was Annie Dillard who said the way we live our moments is the way we live our lives, a reminder for which I'm grateful because when we splice our lives into units like years, months, and weeks, it's easy to let the smaller moments that make up the now slip past us.

Every act of creativity is both cause and effect in our lives—it is the thing we make and a thing (among other influences in our lives) that makes us—it is a very present thing. Past failures from those efforts, especially, are helpful; in many ways they teach us better than success ever could. But together with our triumphs, they are over and the person we were is changed; in effect, gone. Replaced by the person we are now. Failures belong to the person we once were, and so in effect, they belong to another. We take responsibility, we own our flaws, we learn from our mistakes, but we move on. I do not mean that we forget the past, simply that we do not hang on to it, which I'm the first to acknowledge is a fine line. My past is the part of the story I've already written, and I'm grateful for the memories. It's part of my life that no one can take from me, even the failures. I wonder, if we placed more value in our missteps and mistakes, would we live more freely from guilt about them? How would our relationships and our creative lives change with the freedom to be more present?

Neither do we live in the future. Though I don't mean by that that we do not plan, dream, or hope as we look into that direction. The idea that we live as if today were our last has some merits, but if it turns out that we make it into tomorrow, we'll wish we'd given it a little thought. What we do today prepares us for tomorrow, and living an intentional life includes intentional planning. But just as looking back with regret or guilt to a past we can do nothing about is a waste of energy we might better apply to our lives and relationships in the present, so too does worrying about a future that has not come take us out of the moment that is now. If we're not careful, worry and regret will keep us from ever having a present moment, and if Annie Dillard is right about our lives being nothing more than an accumulation of our present moments, then there's a good chance many of us could go our whole lives with very few present moments, and find at the end that we've lived lives that were long but not deep; alive but not living.

In practical terms, the libraries and internet are full of ideas about how to live in the present. But as helpful as all these tips are, they commonly miss a discussion of the very things that stop us from living now. I wish I had something easier to tell you, but I know of only two ideas that take us there: forgiveness and faith. These words carry some baggage, and are often used in a religious context. That's not how I mean them. I think both ideas stand on their own regardless of whether you identify yourself as religious, spiritual, or neither.

Forgiveness is about freedom. You can choose to hang onto guilt or your anger, and you may be justified in doing so. But you can be right or you can be happy. You can live in the present or the past. You can't do both. It's easy to reject forgiveness, easy to hang on because the hurt goes too deep, the offence unforgivable. But that's what forgiveness is for: the unforgivable stuff, the things too painful and evil to imagine. Find a way to forgive (not forget) or don't, but know that clinging to that past prevents us from living in the present. It's our choice. The chains that bind us to our past are only as strong as our grip upon them. Is it easy? Of course not. But forgiveness, whatever it does for others, is a key we use first for our freedom from the tyranny of our past.

Faith is harder to talk about. By faith, I do not mean blind faith that it'll all work out, because it just might not. It might end in tears. It might end worse than that. I used to joke that if 99% of the things we worry about never happen, then clearly worrying works. But it doesn't. It fills us with fear and paralyzes us. It often creates a self-fulfilling loop that's hard to escape. It poisons our art, our relationships, and our lives. Perhaps by faith what I mean is an openness to the possibility that we can handle whatever comes our way. That what doesn't kill us makes us stronger or gives us something to blog about. Faith that while not everything happens for a reason, we can find or make meaning in it, and make our lives and art stronger for it. Faith that pain does not equal harm and that what has been true of every hero in every story since the dawn of time is true for us and that if we triumph we will return a new person. I say "if" because if faith is to have any value at all, it must be honest. And we don't always triumph. And we don't always make it out alive. Even if we live 100 years, there will be one final day in which we breathe our last. But it might come sooner: it's inevitable, inescapable. The moment we accept our mortality we are free from the fear of it, and thus free to live fully in the moment. Our story had a beginning; it will have an end. Have faith that until that end comes, we are not powerless in the writing of our own story.

But what if something horrible happens? I won't be the guy that tells you it won't. It might. Something horrible happens in every great story. That's life. It's what we've got. We've also got the will and the creativity to fight that something horrible, to make art of our struggle, to laugh honest laughter and cry honest tears in its presence. Wishing for safety won't bring it. The present is the only time guaranteed to us to live our lives and make our art. All we have is now.

TOWARD MASTERY

I'm uncomfortable with the word "mastery" in the same way some are uncomfortable with calling themselves an artist. The word itself implies a pinnacle, and I get nervous about heights these days. But as an artist and a human being, I hope all the same that I'm on a *journey* towards mastery of the tools of my craft, and of my own life. Whether I get there is, I think, a matter of perspective, but it's not what matters most to me. It's the journey that matters. There may not even be a destination.

I do not practice Zen, but I see something beautiful in Zen teaching, particularly where that teaching offers wisdom about living in the present and learning to see. There's a word used in Zen teaching: shoshin. It means "beginners mind" and reflects an internal posture towards life, a way of thinking. It says that the mind of the one who believes himself to have arrived, to have become an expert or master in something, is closed to possibility because by definition he believes there remains nothing to learn. It is the learner—the acolyte—who believes that no matter how much he learns, there is always more. So if we walk this long path to mastery only to come to a place where we learn there is much more to learn, the journey is more a cycle than a line. That gives me great hope.

As a photographer, my art doesn't come from the camera. It comes when I'm open and receptive enough to life that I see moments for what they are instead of what I wish them to be. There's a kind of humility towards life that is necessary, a willingness to suspend my own expectations of what will happen, and watch it as it unfolds. The expectations and sense of what *should* happen only blind me to what is. The more I let go, the more I see, and with greater clarity when not seen through the filter of those expectations.

When we think we know what's coming, we prepare to react, and often set ourselves into motion prematurely. We commit to a course of action that's hard to back out of, mentally or emotionally, and we lose the freedom to react with clear intent to what actually comes our way. Being present and receptive—keeping a beginner's mind—are the eyes with which we see as we walk toward mastery.

There's a beautiful Zen tale told of a farmer who, together with his horse, had worked the land for years. One day that horse disappeared and his neighbours came to him to console him. "This is terrible," they said.

"Maybe," was the farmer's reply.

The next day the horse returned, and with it brought three wild horses. The farmer's friends were astonished. "This is amazing!" they said, "How wonderful!"

The farmer replied, "Maybe."

The next day the farmer's son fell from one of the wild horses while trying to tame it, and in his fall broke his leg. "This is terrible," the friends lamented.

Again, the farmer's reply was, "Maybe."

The next day the army marched past, looking to draft young men. They passed by the boy, unable to serve because of his broken leg. Again the friends chimed in and told him how lucky he was.

"Maybe," said the farmer.

This story makes the farmer seem emotionally indifferent, but I think we can chalk that up to a cultural difference and the reason for which the story was told. The lesson is that we see what we want (or expect) to see, and if we suspend our expectations, we see more clearly. The first work of the photographer is not to use the camera, but to see; it's the same for the artist, the poet, the father, and the entrepreneur. Our lives, and our art, are more free and intentional when we hold our expectations with an open hand and see with greater receptivity.

I WILL

I told her I had a few things left on my bucket list. She told me my life *was* a bucket list. I pulled my pen from my pocket, scribbled that down in my dog-eared little notebook. It seemed clever at the time. Like that one time when a friend told me she thought of me as Indiana Jones with a camera, a thought that made me smile for a week. Who doesn't love Indiana Jones?

What makes me recall these details so fondly is that I, of course, want these fantasies to be true as much as anyone else does. I'm surrounded by friends who are one martini away from being James Bond, or one adventure short of being Ernest Shackleton. My friends are hard to connect with. It's recently taken me a couple weeks to get something I needed from a friend because he's been in Antarctica, and the window was tight because he was on his way to Iceland. And when it's not them, it's me; there's as much a chance of us meeting in an airport somewhere on the other side of the globe than here at home. Home is a transferable concept, most of the time. But it's an intoxicating way to live when that same poison doesn't kill you. I don't know one of us who, living this kind of life, wouldn't claim to be the luckiest man or woman on the planet, and I don't know one of us who hasn't been told so a hundred times.

So it makes it hard, when you feel so lucky, so truly kissed by fortune, to have to waver a little and place credit where credit is due: not entirely with fortune, as grateful as we are for her brilliant, meddling ways, but squarely on our own shoulders. It makes it hard because no one likes feeling cocky or ungrateful.

But putting aside for a moment the fact that all of us live our lives floating on a raft that rides the waves and currents of circumstances over which we do not have full, if any, control, it's the foolish traveler who doesn't fashion a rudder to do whatever he can to get where he longs to go. The great American thinker Henry David Thoreau said the mass of men lead lives of quiet desperation. I think they just feel lost on the raft, desperate because the current is too strong, the waves too big, and it's never occurred to them to make a rudder and push across the current. It's never occurred to them to instead live a life of desperate intention.

When you awaken to the truly heartbreaking brevity of life, your heart quickens. It's easy to tape Carpe Diem to your wall, or jot in your journal Mark Twain's encouragement to throw off the bowlines and sail away from safe harbour. But without intention, it will fade, and the boat will stay safe in the harbour. Without action, we don't so much seize the day as slap it on the shoulder as it passes us by.

I don't think we're fundamentally lazy. I don't think it's that so many of us don't make it from re-Tweeting extraordinary quotes to living extraordinary lives just because we never got around to it. I think many of us don't know what's possible, let alone permitted. Raised in a culture that honours the patterns, we went to school, got a job, got married and had kids, and it's only somewhere after that that our souls begin to ask if there weren't other options we might have taken. And now we feel stuck, constrained. If only people would live their lives as creatively and intentionally as they create their art. But then maybe it feels safer to take a risk or two with art than it does with our families, our finances, our futures.

No, the reason so many never got around to it, I think, is because they never knew they had the option. And now they feel stuck. If only they had some notion of how easily we could all climb out of debt if our appetites shrunk. It's not the want of big screen televisions and new cars that is the problem, it's that we want them more than the life we're always telling others we wished we could live. We want to go to India but it seems so far off. Easier to spend $2000 on a new laptop, the one we think we'll need to write our novel when we one day get around to going to India. Except that the new laptop just put India so much further away. It's not wanting this bigger life that is the problem, it's that we're choosing a smaller one every day by the accumulation of little compromises and thoughtless activities that, by now, feel like a rut, and we can't have both. We never knew the other was so possible.

But it is. Most of my friends right now are somewhere amazing on the planet, doing something astonishing, and they're just like you and I. Like you, they struggle sometimes to pay the bills. They have kids and families. They have the same fears and health concerns. Yet there they are. Mongolia. Antarctica. Venice. In the coming year and a half I'll spend time with grizzly bears in British Columbia, and polar bears on Hudson Bay. I'll photograph the snowbound landscapes of Hokkaido, Japan, and the nomadic pastoralists in northern Kenya before coming home to spend a week dogsledding on Baffin Island, then diving with whale sharks in Mexico. And the dirty little secret is—you can do this too, or whatever your version is. You can. And you're either choosing not to, for a million reasons, or you're choosing to do something else. But it's a choice all the same.

There is so much power in the human will. I don't want to make this seem so simple that I'm called out for being a dreamer, but it's amazing what happens when you look at the calendar a year from now and, with a red marker, put a line through three weeks and make a plan. Set a budget. Save your money. Make sacrifices. Sell something you don't use. Put off replacing that iPhone (tech is the worst way to spend money). Put 10% aside faithfully. Tighten the belt. Book the flights on points or start looking for seat sales. Cut the grocery bill by 20% and get creative with lentils and beans. Much of the world lives on a fraction of what we do.

I know. Before you say it, I know. This isn't realistic. You're right, it's not. And it's not realistic for me, either. It never has been. Not for any of us. And most people that have lived their short lives on their own terms have been told so time and time again. But still they do it. They find a way. They find creative ways around the troubling persistence of reality, their doubts, fears, and whatever constraints they have. They don't wait until conditions are perfect.

Conditions are never perfect. It could be they fail nine out of ten times every time they decide to cross the threshold of that next brilliant adventure. But they do it, don't they? And when they don't, when it all goes south, they have stories, not excuses. The year after my accident in Italy I still managed to set foot on six continents while nursing broken feet in the process of healing. I wasn't brave, and I wasn't stupid. I was just stubborn. I want to see this astonishingly beautiful planet and all her surprises, and I'll crawl to see them if I have to.

Whatever your next big adventure—raising your kids, launching your business, seeing the world—do it intentionally. Do it with boldness. Sacrifice what you have to. Cut off the prevailing voices that tell you how impossible it is. It's why I stopped watching television: too many advertisements telling me what I needed to live the good life. Those voices will tell you that you can have anything you want, as long as it's a car, something shiny that the neighbours don't have yet, or anything else, as long as it keeps you shackled to the job that's slowly digesting your soul. I know what I need to live a good life, and it won't be found on television. The story that means the most to me will not be acted, but lived. I don't want to watch *Indiana Jones*. I want to *be* Indiana Jones (or my aging version of it). I promise you, it is possible, but it won't happen accidentally. It happens intentionally, with many a failure. As beautiful as the words "I wish" are, they're impotent next to the words "I will...."

RIPPLES

I could have called this book *A Beautiful Democracy,* but as beautiful as the idea of democracy is, it's a poor fit for the creative life; who we are and what we create is not a matter of majority rule. No one else gets to cast a deciding vote. Our lives together, in community, rely on interdependence and kindness, respect, and often, compromise. But who we are at our core, and what we believe about our calling—our life's true work— is something only we can know, subject as it is to a voice only we can hear. Democracy *depends* on a population that lives like this; it is the only way a vote is meaningful. To merely be a sheep and vote as you're told is not democracy; it's tyranny.

That said, if all these many words have encouraged you to set out, the world be damned, on your own, without others, then I've placed too great an emphasis on the individual aspects of this beautiful anarchy, and I owe

you both an apology and a clarification. None of us can do it all on our own. Owning your own soul, and living in freedom and intent, is not the same thing as living only for, and by, yourself. You can create a life with and for others without losing your will and your soul, but I'm not sure the opposite is true. The life created purely for ourselves withers. Life is for sharing. We are better when we work together, when we help—and allow ourselves to be helped by—others. We are better when what we create ripples outward to touch other lives. And we are richer when we allow our shores to be touched by the ripples of others.

Whatever your work, make it art. Do it with all your heart. Fill your canvas with paint. Let it be messy. Make it bold. Make it unapologetically yours. Most of all: make it.

ABOUT THE AUTHOR

David duChemin is a photographer, writer, and adventurer based in Victoria, Canada, on those rare months he's home. His best-selling books on the art of photography have been translated into a dozen languages, almost none of which he speaks. David is a passionate advocate of the intentional life. When he was a kid his mother told him to leave the world a better place. He's still working on that.

You can find David online at davidduchemin.com.